# IN LOVE

## with Squares & Rectangles

10 Quilt Projects with Batiks & Solids
from Blue Underground Studios

Amy Walsh and Janine Burke

C&T PUBLISHING

Text and Artwork copyright © 2013 by Amy Walsh and Janine Burke

Photography copyright © 2013 by C&T Publishing, Inc.

Publisher: Amy Marson

Creative Director: Gailen Runge

Art Director: Kristy Zacharias

Editor: Lynn Koolish

Technical Editors: Sandy Peterson and Gailen Runge

Cover/Book Designer: April Mostek

Production Coordinator: Jessica Jenkins

Production Editor: Alice Mace Nakanishi

Illustrator: Amy Walsh

Photo Assistant: Cara Pardo

Photography by Christina Carty-Francis and Diane Pedersen of C&T Publishing, Inc., unless otherwise noted

Published by C&T Publishing, Inc., P.O. Box 1456, Lafayette, CA 94549

Library of Congress Cataloging-in-Publication Data

Walsh, Amy (Amy Simpson)

In love with squares & rectangles : 10 quilt projects with Batiks & solids from blue underground studios / Amy Walsh and Janine Burke.

pages cm

ISBN 978-1-60705-643-0 (soft cover)

1. Patchwork quilts. 2. Patchwork--Patterns. 3. Quilting--Patterns. 4. Square in art. 5. Rectangles in art. I. Burke, Janine. II. Title. III. Title: In love with squares and rectangles.

TT835.W337333 2013

746.46--dc23

2012038757

Printed in China

10 9 8 7 6 5 4 3 2 1

## Dedications

**To my parents:**
Thanks for your constant
encouragement!
—*Amy*

**To Amy:**
Thank you for making
this book possible.
—*Janine*

## Acknowledgments

**Thanks to the entire Simpson family**
for your feedback, advice,
and hours of babysitting!

**Sean Walsh,**
thanks *again!*

**Jeanette Lone,**
thanks for quilting, proofing,
and cheerleading.

**Thanks to Nancy Griffin
and Celeste Akre**
for the beautiful bindings.

**Thanks to Anne Davidson**
for your beautiful quilting!

**Thanks to Susanne Woods,**
who helped us get the book
up and running.

**Special thanks to C&T Publishing—**
especially Lynn Koolish,
Sandy Peterson, Alice Mace Nakanishi,
Jessica Jenkins, Diane Peterson,
Cara Pardo, and April Mostek.

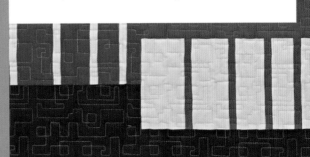

# Contents

# Introduction:
## The Case for Squares and Rectangles

### by Amy Walsh

People often ask us if we get tired of making quilts out of squares and rectangles. The answer is a resounding *no!* If you love fabric as much as we do, sewing straightforward patterns with simple lines is the most direct and fastest way to get from having yardage to having a finished quilt. Many people think that only beginners sew quilts with squares and rectangles. *Not true!* When you make a quilt in which the piecing does not give you angst, you are free to explore many possibilities with color, different types of fabrics and prints, different block sizes and layouts, and so on. These quilts can be achieved with a minimum of fuss in terms of materials. You need only the basics, an adventurous spirit, *and* an open mind.

If we have learned anything in our years of designing and publishing patterns, it is that most quilters have a desire to branch out, explore things outside of their comfort zone, and create works of art that reflect their personality. Janine and I are constantly looking at our environment and auditioning elements for possible patterns. I find, however, that I am more apt to make a pattern out of a variation of something I have seen. In this same spirit, we meet many quilters who express a desire to change patterns. They'll frequently ask us if we'd be offended if they set the blocks differently or change a square block into a rectangular block. We're never offended by a "morph" of our designs. In this book, we've tried to provide you with not only inspiration in the form of finished quilts but also the tools needed to make these quilts your own. Use the color and design information, as well as the variations provided at the end of each chapter, to make changes as you see fit.

# Choosing Fabrics

## Color: A Crash Course

We meet many quilters who say that when it comes to color, they haven't a clue. Some tell us they are in the habit of buying kits so that they do not have to make fabric choices themselves. Others confess to using fabrics from a single line so that they "know" each fabric will go with the others.

Choosing fabrics and working with color is, in our opinion, one of the most enjoyable and rewarding parts of the quiltmaking process. Knowing a little bit about color theory and how to apply it to quilting is very helpful and can go a long way toward the process of learning to work with color intuitively. If you do not have any books on color (they do not necessarily have to be written for quilters), consider adding some to your library. We've listed some of our favorites in Resources (page 70). Below is some basic information to get you started.

### The Color Wheel

The three *primary colors* are red, yellow, and blue. On the color wheel, the *secondary colors* (orange, green, and violet) are between the primary colors, and the *tertiary colors*, such as red-violet and blue-violet, are between the primary and secondary colors. Each of the primary, secondary, and tertiary colors can have many tints and shades. When working with fabrics, it is important to be able to recognize tints and shades of each color.

The color wheel also organizes the colors in such a way that it is easy to determine formal color relationships. For example, *complementary colors* are those that appear across from each other on the color wheel. Violet and yellow, orange and blue, and red and green are all examples of complementary color schemes. When used together, complementary colors create drama and contrast. You can manipulate the look of a complementary color scheme by changing the amount of each color that you use.

The yellow-orange and cerulean blue complementary colors are high contrast and high impact, as are the violet and yellow in *Square Dance* (page 55).

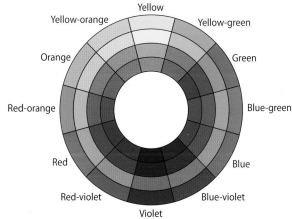

Color wheel

*Analogous colors* are those that appear next to each other on the color wheel. An example of an analogous palette is red-orange, red, and red-violet; another is yellow-green, green, and blue-green. These color schemes can often be a little less dramatic than the complementary colors and sometimes even soothing, depending on the degree of intensity of the fabrics you are working with.

Having a color wheel at your disposal can make identifying and pairing colors much easier. You will find yourself internalizing information about color as you use the wheel to make color choices. If you are really ambitious, tackle making your own color wheel. Make one out of the obvious choice—fabric. Don't worry about sewing it together—just glue or pin your fabrics to a piece of neutral-colored poster board. Again, you will find yourself internalizing color relationships and terminology when using the fabrics in your own stash. Even if you don't use it formally, it will help your color work in the long run. And it can also help you determine areas of your stash that need work. For example, I am *never* short on fabrics in the green and blue color families. I am forever short on oranges and yellows. If you take the time to go through your stash to make a color wheel, you will have to look at all your fabrics based on the color family

This analogous variation of *Cornerstones* (page 38) provides a soothing look.

they belong in as opposed to the type of fabric, the manufacturer, or the genre.

Working with color and improving your color sense is a long process, so don't be discouraged if you are not satisfied with your first attempts to formally use color theory in your quiltmaking. As you increase your skill, you will find yourself making intuitive color choices, so keep at it. Sometimes you may even prefer your intuitive quilts to those you have formally planned.

## Cool and Warm Colors

Colors can also be classified as cool or warm. Typically, warm colors include red, orange, yellow, and fuchsia. Cool colors include green, blue, and teal. We have found that violet can be classified as either, depending on its surroundings. Colors can evoke emotions and also set the overall tone for a quilt project. Cool colors tend to be more serene and restful than warmer colors. However, they also tend to feel less warm. This may seem like an obvious statement, but it's so true.

Variation of *Square Dance* (page 55) in cool blues

In Love with Squares & Rectangles

*Fast Lane* (page 29) alternative colorway, combining warm and cool colors

As a general rule of thumb, warm colors tend to pop out and cool colors tend to recede. This is an important rule to remember when you are using a mixed palette. If you are working with greens, reds, blues, and oranges together, knowing that the blues and greens will recede can help you keep a balanced amount of each fabric color in your project.

You will find as you are working with color that value and classification are relative. Colors can behave differently depending on the colors that they are "working with." As a general rule, you can assume that if a color is surrounded by its direct complement, it will really stand out. If it is surrounded by colors near to it on the color wheel, it will appear to be more subtle.

Purple fabric surrounded by yellow fabric (direct complements)

Purple fabric surrounded by blue fabric (analogous colors)

Blue can appear to have a violet undertone when surrounded by red. Surrounding colors can also make a color appear lighter or darker. The same shade of red will look a lot brighter if it is surrounded by pink or yellow than if it is surrounded by blue or green.

Blue fabric surrounded by red fabric

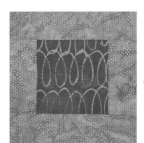

Blue fabric surrounded by green fabric

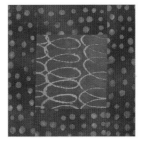

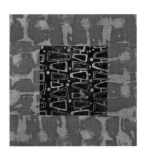

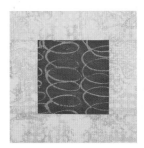

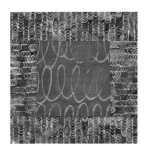

Red fabric surrounded by different colors

## Color Intensity

In addition to knowing how different colors behave on their own and with other colors, it is important to have an idea of color intensity. This is sometimes referred to as the degree of saturation of a color, or put quite simply, how bright it is. Mixing fabrics of all degrees of saturation will sometimes be appropriate (as in *Bamboo*, page 24, or *Berry Patch*, page 14). Other times, you will find that you want to use fabrics with only one degree of saturation (such as in *Fast Lane*, page 29, or *Square Dance*, page 55). In many cases, choosing the degree of saturation in your quilt fabrics is simply a matter of personal taste. Fabrics that are more saturated are often referred to as *brights*. You may find that these more saturated fabrics are not to your taste specifically when they are on their own. Try putting a few in your next quilt—you may find that you like the spice they add to your project.

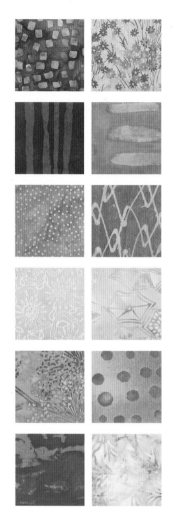

*Left:* Saturated (bright) fabrics
*Right:* Less-saturated fabrics

## What about Black and White?

Black and white are colors that do not even appear on the color wheel but are often the ones we turn to as neutrals or background fabrics. These can be very helpful when you want high contrast (as in *Fast Lane*, page 29, and *Square Dance*, page 55). As quilters, we are often drawn to colored prints and rarely work with black and white. Adding black and white to your quilts, whether as prints or solids, can be quite striking. Black often creates a feeling of mystery or drama. When used with muted colors, black can create a very dark-looking quilt. When used with bright, saturated colors, black can provide the contrast needed to make these colors stand out. White has the opposite effect of black in a quilt. It can make a quilt appear light and airy—and I'd even venture to say friendly. The use of white prints in *Sky Blue* (page 42) gives the quilt a very carefree and happy look. Even if you are not drawn specifically to black or white, try adding some to your stash and working these fabrics into some of your future quilts.

Original *Berry Patch* (page 14) colors

This variation of *Berry Patch* is an excellent example of using black-and-white prints.

Original *Bamboo* colors

*Bamboo* using large-scale prints in analogous colors

## Assembling a Palette

Often, it makes sense to start a quilt with a specific color in mind, especially if the quilt pattern you want to use is shown in a monochromatic (single-color) or analogous palette. Take *Bamboo* (page 24), for instance. Green may not be your color of choice for this quilt—perhaps you want to make it in reds and pinks. Your intuition will guide your color decisions. Or if you have a favorite print that you have wanted to use, you may decide to pull one or more colors directly from that print to start your color palette.

Don't forget—your decisions are not set in stone. It is never too late to change course while you are making a quilt.

*Bamboo* using lively warm prints

*Bamboo* in cool analogous colors

# Design Decisions

## Customizing a Design

Just because you are using a pattern does not mean you can't make a quilt your own. Sometimes designing a quilt from scratch can be a rather daunting proposition. Altering an existing pattern, however, is an entirely different story. When you are sewing a quilt from a pattern, you can customize it to fit your needs and your individual design sensibilities in several ways—besides changing the colors. You may find that you want to make a quilt smaller or larger without changing the number of blocks. You might be drawn to the style of a block but not the layout of the overall quilt. Or, you may just want to give a quilt your own personal touch. Knowing some basics about pattern design can help you make these decisions.

### Block Settings

Most quilt patterns use block repetition—that is to say they are made up of one or more blocks repeated at regular intervals. For example, *Berry Patch* (page 14) is made entirely of one block, repeated in nine rows of nine blocks each. Knowledge of even this basic information can guide your decision to make changes in a pattern. You can change a couple things about a pattern with very little effort. Try adding alternate blocks. These can be plain blocks, cut the same size as the pieced blocks, or pieced blocks of a completely different pattern. Or, try adding negative space. You can piece fewer blocks than the quilt calls for and add sashing and/or a wide border. The blocks will appear as if they are floating. You can also change the layout of the quilt blocks. The following are some options for arranging finished quilt blocks.

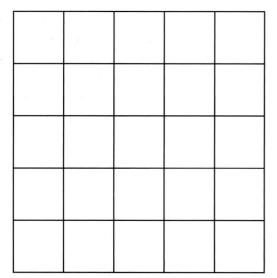

**Straight lines (square grid):** This is perhaps the most common way of setting quilt blocks—in rows, with blocks (rectangular or square) stacked on top of one another.

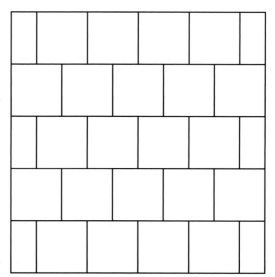

**Brick setting:** Blocks are offset horizontally.

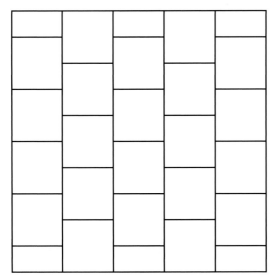

**Vertical brick setting, also known as half-drop:** Blocks are offset vertically.

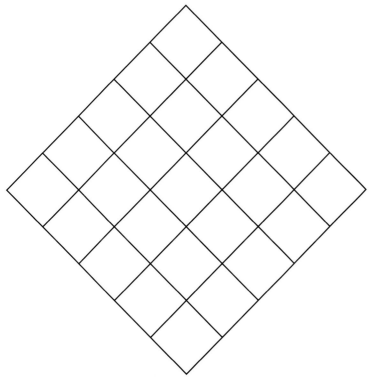

**On point, often called the diamond setting:** Blocks are placed in rows diagonally. This is an obvious choice for square blocks. However, with a little tenacity, rectangular blocks can also be set on point in rows.

Changing the way the blocks themselves are set within the quilt top can change the overall look of the quilt dramatically. And don't forget that all the different options of color schemes, quilting designs, and fabric textures create endless possibilities for you to change the look of your finished project.

# Elements of Design

The basic principles of design apply to art in all forms—painting, textile design, drawing, and so on. A basic knowledge of some of the elements of design makes it easier for you to change and adapt the designs of your quilts. The following are principles that we use all the time as quilters but rarely take the time to think about. When we started becoming aware of these principles, we saw our design sensibilities changing.

## Line

As quiltmakers, we work with two-dimensional shapes. The edges of the shapes that we use (in the case of Blue Underground Studios, primarily squares and rectangles) begin to form some of the basic *lines* in our patterns. The arrangement of blocks also plays an integral part in the lines that are formed within a pattern. And we would be remiss if we did not mention the quilting as part of the equation here. By manipulating thread and pattern choices when we quilt, we can further change the lines within the quilt pattern.

## Shape

For the purposes of most quiltmakers, *shapes* are geometric shapes, created by lines. The repetition of shapes is what creates quilt patterns.

### Direction

In a quilt, *direction* is the way in which the blocks are placed—again, a distinct design decision. You might decide on the direction of quilt blocks based on what is more pleasing to your eye at the time. Other times, it is the idea behind the quilt that guides this decision. Either way, direction is a fun element to manipulate.

### Size and Scale

Both *size* and *scale* refer to the actual size of the quilt pieces relative to each other. You can change the size of a block to achieve a particular look. Or you might change the size for the sake of practicality. For example, if you want to make a small wallhanging out of a pattern for a queen-size quilt, you may choose to change the size of the blocks in addition to or instead of changing the number of blocks you make. Remember: When you are changing block size, the proportions of each piece within the block will affect the design or look of the quilt.

### Color

*Color* is so important that it has its own section in this book (see Color: A Crash Course, pages 5–8). Always keep in mind that color is critical to the overall success of a design.

### Texture

*Texture* refers to the overall surface quality of the quilt created by the blocks, the quilting patterns, and the fabrics. Solid fabrics will not add texture to a quilt design, which is the main reason we like to quilt our solid quilts very closely. Batiks and printed fabrics, however, offer the opportunity to add and vary textures throughout a quilt top.

## Making Design Decisions

As you are beginning a quilt top, all the decisions you make, even from the very beginning when you are pulling fabrics out of your stash or shopping for a new palette, will start to dictate the overall look of the finished project.

Familiarizing yourself with basic color and design theory will help you to anticipate the impact of your decisions. Do not be intimidated by this prospect! There is no harm in aimlessly sewing, or choosing a pattern with the express purpose of avoiding design decisions altogether. Sometimes it is nice to let someone else do all of the work for you. Nevertheless, it is nice to know that as a quilt artist, you can empower yourself to make design decisions that influence your finished work.

For each pattern in *In Love with Squares & Rectangles*, we've included suggestions for altering the look of the featured quilt. This is meant to be a springboard for your imagination. There are countless ways to alter each of the quilts featured. Feel free to use one (or more) of the suggestions, as well as come up with your own.

PROJECTS

# Berry Patch

*Berry Patch,* machine pieced and quilted by Amy Walsh

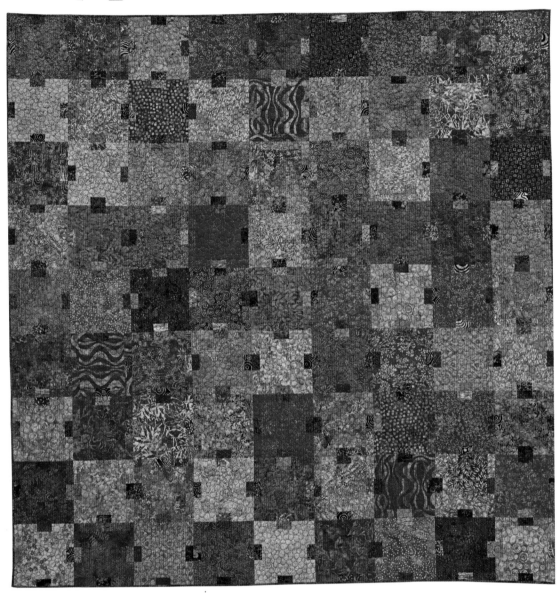

**FINISHED BLOCK SIZE: 8″ × 8″** • **FINISHED QUILT SIZE: 72″ × 72″**

Over the years, I have learned a lot about color and how to use it to manipulate the look of a quilt. Lately, I have been particularly drawn to monochromatic and analogous palettes. I also have grown to appreciate working with palettes that are a little out of my comfort zone. Pink and purple are not necessarily colors that I wake up in the morning thinking about. However, I love the way they come together in this quilt!

By the way, don't skimp on fabrics for this quilt—the greater the variety of batiks, the more depth and movement the quilt will have!

## MATERIALS

*The yardage given here makes a twin-size quilt. Refer to Alternate Sizes and Yardage Requirements (page 17) for other sizes and fabric requirements.*

**Assorted pink/fuchsia batiks:** 27 strips 7″ × 40″ or 5½ yards total (*Note:* Each strip will yield enough pieces for 3 *Berry Patch* blocks.)

**Assorted purple/plum batiks:** 13 strips 2½″ × 40″ or 1 yard total

**Backing:** 4⅝ yards (41″ wide)

**Batting:** 82″ × 82″

**Binding:** ⅝ yard

 **TIP** We usually prewash our batik fabrics to get rid of any residue that may be left from the production process. We have found that this step makes quilting the top a lot more pleasant.

## CUTTING

**Cut from assorted pink/fuchsia batiks:**
- 27 strips 7″ × 40″

Subcut each strip into:

3 squares 6½″ × 6½″ (Unit D)

12 rectangles 1½″ × 2½″ (Unit B)

12 rectangles 1½″ × 3½″ (Unit C)

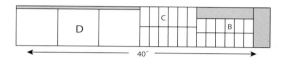

**Cut from assorted purple/plum batiks:**
- 13 strips 2½″ × 40″

Subcut each strip into 26 rectangles 1½″ × 2½″ (Unit A).

# Piecing and Pressing

To make the quilt as shown, you will need to make a total of 81 *Berry Patch* blocks. Refer to Alternate Sizes and Yardage Requirements (page 17) for additional sizes and block requirements.

Each *Berry Patch* block uses 4 Unit A pieces from the various purple/plum batiks; and 4 Unit B pieces, 4 Unit C pieces, and 1 Unit D piece from a single pink/fuchsia batik.

**1.** Sew a Unit B piece to both sides of a Unit A piece. Press the seams open. Repeat to make 2.

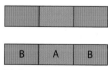

Make 2.

**2.** Sew a Unit C piece to both sides of a Unit A piece. Press the seams open. Repeat to make 2.

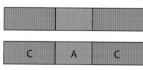

Make 2.

**3.** Sew a completed A/B unit to both sides of the center square D. Press the seams open.

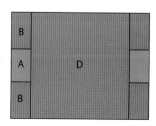

**4.** Sew a completed A/C unit to the top and bottom of the unit from Step 3. Press the seams open. The raw blocks measure 8½˝ × 8½˝.

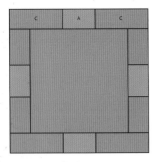

**5.** Repeat Steps 1–4 to make 81 blocks.

> **TIP** A good ¼˝ seam is extremely important for this block. If the seams are off, you may have trouble sewing the blocks together when you are ready to complete the quilt top. Before you begin sewing, be sure to test the accuracy of your seam and adjust as necessary.

# Quilt Top Construction

**1.** Arrange the blocks in 9 rows of 9 blocks each. Balance the different shades and textures throughout so that the viewer's eye is constantly moving across the quilt top.

**2.** When you find an arrangement you like, sew the blocks together in rows, pressing the seams open as you sew.

**3.** Sew together the rows, pressing the seams open.

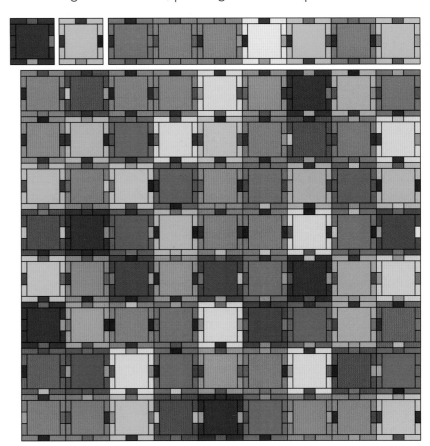

Quilt assembly diagram

# Finishing

*Refer to Quiltmaking Basics (pages 62–69) for specifics on layering, quilting, and binding the quilt.*

I quilted *Berry Patch* with an allover freehand stone meander. It is very densely quilted to add plenty of texture. I usually choose a thread that will blend in with the fabrics. However, in this particular case, the quilting really keeps the berry theme of the top going, so I chose a dark blue-gray thread. The blue tone of the thread picks up the blue tones in both the purple and pink batiks I used in the top.

*Berry Patch* has a straight-grain binding. It is attached by machine and finished by hand.

## Alternate Sizes and Yardage Requirements

| Quilt size | Block set | Number of blocks | Minimum number of 7″ × 40″ pink/fuchsia batik strips | Minimum number of 2½″ × 40″ purple/plum batik strips | Backing | Batting | Binding |
|---|---|---|---|---|---|---|---|
| Baby/wall 32″ × 32″ | 4 × 4 | 16 | 6 | 3 | 1¼ yard (42″ wide minimum) | 42″ × 42″ | ⅜ yard |
| Throw 48″ × 48″ | 6 × 6 | 36 | 12 | 6 | 3¼ yards | 58″ × 58″ | ½ yard |
| Queen 96″ × 96″ | 12 × 12 | 144 | 48 | 23 | 8⅞ yards | 106″ × 106″ | ⅞ yard |
| King 120″ × 120″ | 15 × 15 | 225 | 75 | 35 | 10⅞ yards (44″ wide) | 130″ × 130″ | 1⅛ yards |

## Shake It Up!

You can drastically change the look of *Berry Patch* by using one or more of the following options.

Try setting the blocks on point. You may need to make more blocks to get the quilt size you are after, but the results are worth it! We've also changed the color scheme for this example, using bright, saturated batiks in place of the pinks/fuchsias and dark blue in place of the plum.

Completely change the color palette. In this example, we used blacks and whites for high contrast. The red used for the small squares adds a fun pop to this classic color combination.

Try offsetting the blocks. Again, you will need to make more blocks to get the quilt to the size you need, but the quilt will look completely different.

# Echo

*Echo*, machine pieced by Janine Burke, machine quilted by Ann Davidson

**FINISHED BLOCK SIZE: 12″ × 6″** • **FINISHED QUILT SIZE: 84″ × 90″**

During my childhood, I spent a lot of time in the Colorado Rockies with my family. Crisp, clear, cloudless days were ideal for being outside. There's a silence to the world up there that is a wonder to experience. My cousins and I would stand in a snowy valley, and one of us would yell out our name or simply yell, "Hello." Then we would just stand there and listen to the echo as it went on for miles. This design and color palette is my version of those echoes we created during the days of our youth.

## MATERIALS

*The yardage given here makes a double-size quilt. Refer to Alternate Sizes and Yardage Requirements (page 22) for other sizes and yardage requirements.*

**Echo blocks:**

Medium gray solid: ½ yard

Coordinating solids: ½ yard each of 4 different colors or 2 yards total

White solid: 2½ yards

**Spacers:**

Light gray solid: 1¼ yards

Medium gray solid: 1¼ yards

Dark gray solid: 1¼ yards

Backing: 7⅞ yards

Batting: 94″ × 100″

Binding: ⅞ yard

 **TIP** I used the same medium gray solid for both the *Echo* blocks and the spacers.

## CUTTING

**Cut from each 1¼-yard solid (light, medium, and dark gray):**

• 3 strips 12½″ × 40″

Subcut each strip into 6 rectangles 6½″ × 12½″. (*Note:* These rectangles will be the spacers between the *Echo* blocks. Set these aside for when you are ready to lay out the blocks. There are 2 extra.)

**Cut from each ½-yard solid (1 medium gray and 4 colors):**

• 1 strip 3½″ × 40″

• 1 strip 3″ × 40″

• 1 strip 2½″ × 40″

• 1 strip 2″ × 40″

• 1 strip 1½″ × 40″

• 4 strips 1″ × 40″

**Cut from white solid:**

• 5 strips 3½″ × 40″

• 5 strips 3″ × 40″

• 5 strips 2½″ × 40″

• 5 strips 2″ × 40″

• 5 strips 1½″ × 40″

• 20 strips 1″ × 40″

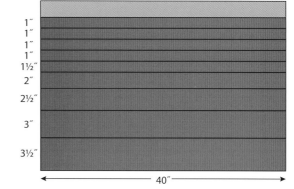

---

# Piecing and Pressing

The blocks for *Echo* are constructed by making strata or strip-pieced units. Make a total of 10 strata: 5 strata with color-based backgrounds (from the coordinating solids plus medium gray) and 1″ white accent stripes, and 5 "reversed" with white-based backgrounds and 1″ color accent stripes.

**1.** Using the 5 various-width strips of a solid color and 4 white 1″-wide stripes, arrange the strips into strata.

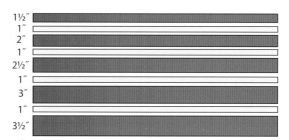

**2.** Sew together the strips in pairs. Press the seams open. Sew together the pairs until all 9 strips are sewn into a unit. Press the seams open.

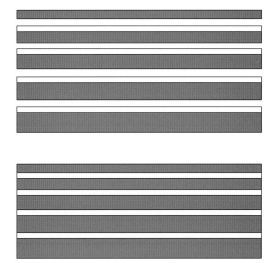

**3.** Repeat Steps 1 and 2 for the various-width strips of each of the color solids and 1˝ white accent stripes as well as for the 5 various-width strips of the white-based strata with the 1˝ color accent stripes.

| **TIP** | The raw strata units measure 12½˝ wide including the seams. If your strata unit measures less than 12½˝, the ¼˝ seam is a thread's width or so too large. If your strata unit measures more than 12½˝, the ¼˝ seam is a thread's width or so too small. Adjust accordingly. |
| --- | --- |

## More Cutting

After you have 10 strata pieced, subcut each into 6½˝ × 12½˝ rectangles. Each strata unit yields 6 *Echo* blocks.

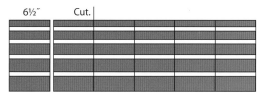

Cut 6 blocks from each strata unit.

## Quilt Top Construction

**1.** Refer to the quilt assembly diagram as necessary to place the *Echo* blocks and spacers into columns. Balance color, gray, and white evenly throughout so that the viewer's eye moves smoothly over the top. There are a few extra strata blocks so you can balance the colors. Note that columns are offset by a half-block on the top and bottom of every other column. Cut these half-blocks to 3½˝ × 12½˝.

**2.** Sew the blocks together into columns. Press the seams open.

**3.** Sew the columns together and press the seams open.

Quilt assembly diagram

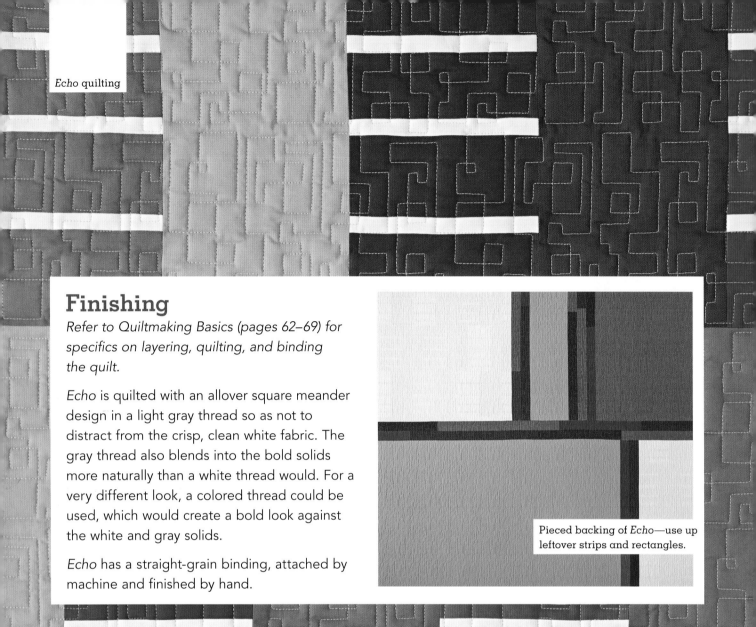

*Echo quilting*

# Finishing

*Refer to Quiltmaking Basics (pages 62–69) for specifics on layering, quilting, and binding the quilt.*

*Echo* is quilted with an allover square meander design in a light gray thread so as not to distract from the crisp, clean white fabric. The gray thread also blends into the bold solids more naturally than a white thread would. For a very different look, a colored thread could be used, which would create a bold look against the white and gray solids.

*Echo* has a straight-grain binding, attached by machine and finished by hand.

Pieced backing of *Echo*—use up leftover strips and rectangles.

## Alternate Sizes and Yardage Requirements

| Quilt size | Number of columns | Number of Echo blocks | Number of strata | Number of ½-yard solids (includes gray) | White yardage | Number of spacers | Number of 12½″ gray strips for spacers | Backing | Batting | Binding |
|---|---|---|---|---|---|---|---|---|---|---|
| Lap/throw 60″ × 66″ | 5 | 30 (15 color-based, 15 white-based) | 6 | 3 | 1½ yards | 27 | 6 (2 each of light, medium, and dark) | 4 yards | 70″ × 76″ | ⅝ yard |
| Queen 90″ × 108″ | 9 | 72 | 12 | 6 | 2⅞ yards | 67 | 12 | 8⅓ yards | 100″ × 118″ | ⅞ yard |

# Shake It Up!

Change the look of *Echo* by using one or more of the following options.

Set the blocks vertically instead of horizontally.

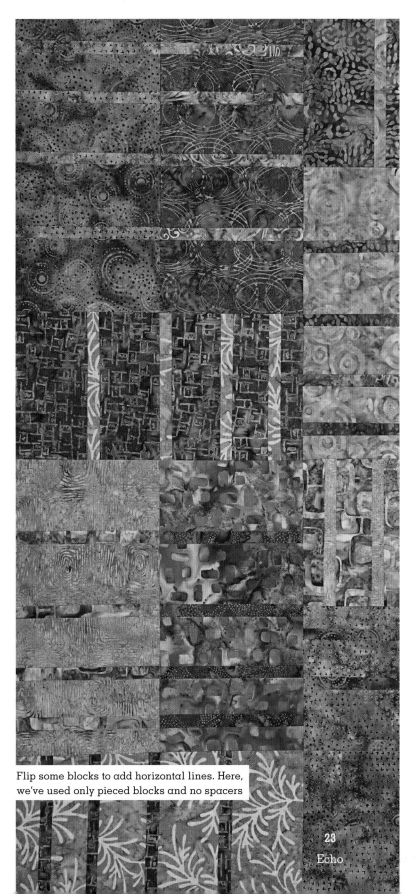

Flip some blocks to add horizontal lines. Here, we've used only pieced blocks and no spacers

Change the palette by removing the color and adding black. Also, the blocks are not offset.

# Bamboo

Bamboo, machine pieced and
machine quilted by Amy Walsh

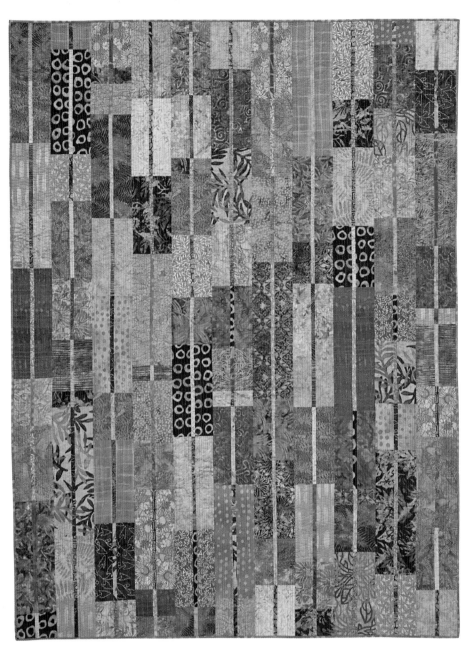

**FINISHED BLOCK SIZE:** 5½˝ × varying lengths
**FINISHED QUILT SIZE:** 60½˝ × 79˝

I love working with an analogous palette almost as much as
I love working with blues and greens. *Bamboo* is a design
that has been swimming around in my head for quite some
time. It was inspired by a quilt of the same name made by
my friend Kathy, who has traveled extensively and visited a
bamboo forest in Asia.

## MATERIALS

*The yardage given here makes a large throw-size quilt. For this project, a fat quarter is assumed to be 17½″ × 21″ and fabric yardage is assumed to be 42″ wide. Refer to Alternate Sizes and Yardage Requirements (page 27) for other sizes and yardage requirements.*

Note: Be sure that you have a wide range of green hues as you begin to cut and piece the *Bamboo* top. If you do not have a wide enough variety of fabrics, you may not be happy with the contrast within each block and between the assembled blocks.

**Assorted green batiks and prints:**
22 fat quarters

> *Alternative:* Use 22 strips 7″ × 42″ of assorted green fabrics from a total of 4½ yards. One fat quarter or 1 strip 7″ × 42″ will yield enough strips for 2 complete *Bamboo* strata (see Piecing and Pressing, at right).

**Backing:** 5 yards

**Batting:** 71″ × 89″

**Binding:** ⅝ yard

> **TIP** We usually prewash our batik fabrics to get rid of any residue that may be left over from the production process. We have found that this step makes quilting the top a lot more pleasant.

## CUTTING

**Cut from assorted green fat quarters:**
- 44 sets of 2 matching strips, each 3″ × 21″ (a total of 88 strips)
- 44 strips 1″ × 21″

> Note: If you are using 42″-wide yardage, cut 44 strips 3″ × 42″ and cut 22 strips 1″ × 42″. Cut each strip crosswise in half to yield 88 strips 3″ × 21″ and 44 strips 1″ × 21″.

## Piecing and Pressing

The units used in *Bamboo* are constructed by making strata, or strip-pieced units.

**1.** Sew matching strips 3″ × 21″ to both sides of a 1″ × 21″ strip (a strip on each side). Press the seams open. The raw strata measure 6″ × 21″. Make 44 strata.

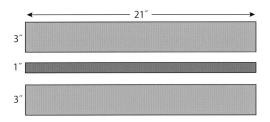

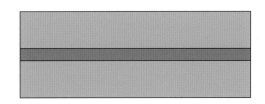

> **TIPS**
>
> • Because the 1″ × 21″ center strip is so narrow, you may find it easier to press the seams if you add one 3″ × 21″ strip to the center strip, press the seams open, and then add the second strip. As is usually the case, a good ¼″ seam here is very important. If your machine's seams are off, you will have trouble lining up the center strips in each block as you sew the blocks together.
>
> • I made about 10 extra strata for the pictured quilt. This allowed me to take out some of the original fabrics I had chosen and replace them with ones that were more fitting.
>
> • Try cutting 5 or 6 strata units at a time. As you cut, you can begin to arrange blocks on a design wall to see how they are coming together. If you find you have too many of one size or color, you can adjust accordingly as you cut the remaining strata.

**2.** Subcut each strata unit into rectangles of various sizes and squares. Resist the urge to cut the same size repeatedly. The lengths of the cut blocks in the pictured quilt are shown on the right (note that all are 6″ wide including their seam allowances).

| 2½″ | 8½″ | 13″ |
|---|---|---|
| 6″ | 10½″ | 15″ |
| 7″ | 12″ | 21″ |

## Quilt Top Construction

**1.** When you have completed the strata and their subcuts, arrange the blocks into 11 vertical rows. Each row should be approximately 79″–85″ in length, depending on the actual usable width of the fat quarters or yardage. You can adjust the rows as needed, moving them up or down, so that the block seams are offset.

**2.** When you find an arrangement that you like, sew the blocks together in vertical rows, pressing the seams open as you sew.

**3.** Sew the rows together, pressing the seams open.

**4.** Trim the top and bottom of the quilt top so that the final vertical measurement is 79″ and the quilt top is square at the corners.

Quilt assembly diagram

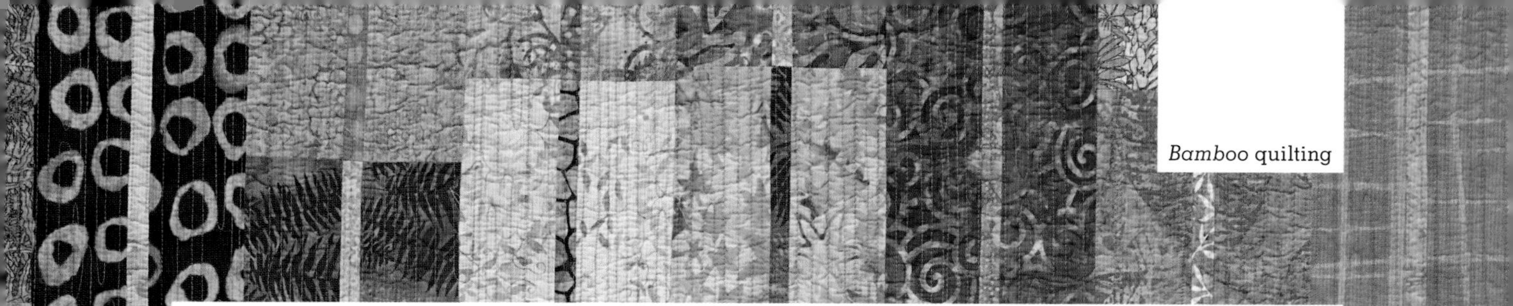

# Finishing

*Refer to Quiltmaking Basics (pages 62–69) for specifics on layering, quilting, and binding the quilt.*

I quilted *Bamboo* on my longarm machine with very long vertical lines. The overall design looks a little like an elongated water meander. I really wanted the quilting to enhance the vertical lines of the quilt, thus completing the basic idea behind it—long lines of natural bamboo. And as you may have guessed, I used thread in a shade of lime green, one of my favorite colors. I especially like it on this quilt because it melts into some of the lighter greens and really pops out on some of the darker shades of green.

*Bamboo* has a straight-grain binding. It is attached by machine and finished by hand.

*Bamboo* can easily be made smaller or larger by changing the vertical dimensions and the number of rows. The chart below suggests some sizes and their yardage requirements.

## Alternate Sizes and Yardage Requirements

| Quilt size | Number of vertical rows | Minimum number of strata | Quilt top yardage requirement | Backing | Batting | Binding |
|---|---|---|---|---|---|---|
| Baby/wall 44″ × 45″ | 8 | 24 | 12 fat quarters (or use 12 strips 7″ × 42″ for a total of 2⅝ yards) | 3 yards | 54″ × 55″ | ½ yard |
| Throw 49½″ × 60″ | 9 | 29 | 15 fat quarters (or use 15 strips 7″ × 42″ for a total of 3¼ yards) | 3⅓ yards | 60″ × 70″ | ⅝ yard |
| Queen 93½″ × 96″ | 17 | 85 | 43 fat quarters (or use 43 strips 7″ × 42″ for a total of 8⅝ yards) | 8⅔ yards | 104″ × 106″ | ⅞ yards |
| King 104½″ × 108″ | 19 | 114 | 57 fat quarters (or use 57 strips 7″ × 42″ for a total of 11⅓ yards) | 9⅝ yards | 115″ × 118″ | 1 yard |

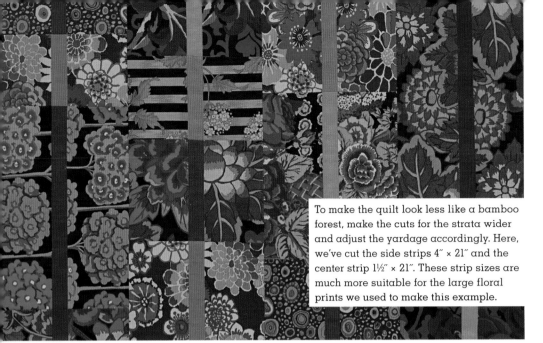

## Shake It Up!

You can change the look of *Bamboo* by using one or more of the following options.

To make the quilt look less like a bamboo forest, make the cuts for the strata wider and adjust the yardage accordingly. Here, we've cut the side strips 4″ × 21″ and the center strip 1½″ × 21″. These strip sizes are much more suitable for the large floral prints we used to make this example.

For a completely different look, subcut the strata to only one size. In this sample, all of the subcuts are 4½″ long to make finished blocks 5½″ × 4″. The vibrant prints also contribute to a look very different from the original.

Use two alternating subcut sizes and set the rows horizontally, as shown here. We chose 2½″ and 5½″ subcuts and used only two batiks for this example. The look is quite striking and completely different from the original.

# Fast Lane

*Fast Lane*, machine pieced by Janine Burke, machine quilted by Ann Davidson

**FINISHED ROW SIZE: 4½″ • FINISHED QUILT SIZE: 76″ × 90″**

Traffic in a multicolored world: millions of people in millions of vehicles, traveling to millions of destinations. Everyone has a place to get to and a story to tell about it. This is my (extremely) scaled-down, colorful version of all those cars and trucks and vans out on the highways and byways of life.

## MATERIALS

*The yardage given here makes a twin-size quilt. The usable width of fabric is assumed to be 40˝, which results in a 76˝ finished quilt width.*

**Bright solids:** 20 strips 9˝ × 40˝ or 5¼ yards total

**White solid:** 1¼ yards

**Backing:** 5⅝ yards (43˝ wide)

**Batting:** 86˝ × 100˝

**Binding:** ⅞ yard

## CUTTING

**Cut from each bright solid strip:**

• 1 strip 5˝ × 40˝

• 2 strips 2˝ × 40˝

**Cut from white solid:**

• 20 strips 2˝ × 40˝

# Piecing and Pressing

The units used in the rows for *Fast Lane* are constructed by making strata, or strip-pieced units.

**NOTE** The randomness of this quilt may prove challenging to some. I cut and pieced the first row randomly and placed it on the floor. From there, I randomly cut the pieced units of the second row and arranged them in relation to the first row so that they were staggered. When I was happy with the placement of the white within the row, I cut the 5˝ solid strip into the necessary lengths and sewed that row together. I made all 20 rows using this method so that the placement of the white was balanced throughout the quilt top.

Most of the rows will have 9 segments (4 pieced units and 5 solid pieces). In a couple rows, I used only 8 segments (4 pieced units and 4 solid pieces) so that I could put a pieced unit on one end or the other. For these rows, you will need to cut an additional ½˝ off of one of the solid pieces in order to keep the measurement of the row consistent with those above and below.

**1.** Using both 2˝ × 40˝ strips of a bright solid, sew a 2˝ × 40˝ strip to either long side of a 2˝ × 40˝ white strip. The raw strata are 5˝ wide.

**2.** Cut the strata from Step 1 into 4 units of random lengths, such as a short rectangle, 2 long rectangles, and a medium rectangle.

**3.** From the 5˝ × 40˝ strip of the same color as the bright solid in Steps 1 and 2, cut 5 random lengths.

**4.** Separate the pieced units with solid pieces and sew them together. Press the seams open.

**5.** Repeat Steps 1–4 to make 20 rows.

## Quilt Top Construction

When you have all the rows sewn into long strips, sew rows to rows, pressing the seams open. Keep the ends of the rows even so you can square up the quilt top and trim it to 76″ × 90″.

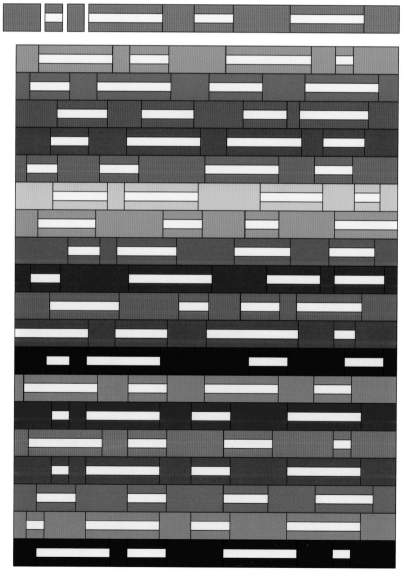

Quilt assembly diagram

# Finishing

*Refer to Quiltmaking Basics (pages 62–69) for specifics on layering, quilting, and binding the quilt.*

*Note:* When working with white and colored fabrics together, be aware of stray colored threads that lie on the back of white fabric. They will be visible from the front, posing a challenge if quilted over. As a longarm quilter, I know how tricky they can be to remove. Even the most diligent quilter can have these varicose threads get caught under white.

*Fast Lane* was quilted with a relatively dense water meander design to give it lots of texture. I chose to use a white thread for its subtlety, as opposed to a bright color.

*Fast Lane* has a straight-grain binding, attached by machine and finished by hand.

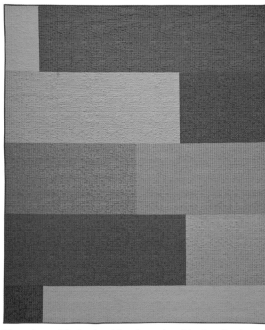

Have fun with the backing by using blocks of color.

# Shake It Up!

Change the look of *Fast Lane* using one or more of the following options.

Give the quilt a fresh look by flipping the colors: Put the colored strips in a field of white.

For a completely different look, change the color palette, put the strips on point, and leave the strata long.

Add "medians" between the rows of traffic.

# All the Above

*All the Above*, machine pieced by Amy Walsh, machine quilted by Ann Davidson

**FINISHED BLOCK SIZE: 6″ × 6″ • FINISHED QUILT SIZE: 90″ × 90″**

I have always loved a basic checkerboard design. This quilt came about one day as I was drawing some checkerboard patterns in my design notebook and trying to find ways to vary them slightly. It's extremely striking and makes a great quilt for guys and girls alike. I happen to love quilts that are constructed with alternate solid blocks. Not only do they look smashing, but they also come together very quickly!

## MATERIALS

*The yardage given here makes a queen-size quilt. Refer to Alternate Sizes and Yardage Requirements (page 36) for other sizes and yardage requirements.*

*Note:* I used 30 of Marcia Derse's prints from Troy fabrics in the pictured quilt to add plenty of color variation.

**Pieced blocks:**

**Assorted prints or colored solids:** 19 strips 2¼″ × 40″ or 1¼ yards

**Cream-colored solid:** 2¾ yards

**Solid alternate blocks:**

**Charcoal gray solid:** 3⅝ yards

**Backing:** 8⅓ yards

**Batting:** 100″ × 100″

**Binding:** ⅞ yard

## CUTTING

**Cut from assorted prints or batiks:**
- 19 strips 2¼″ × 40″

Subcut each strip into 6 rectangles 2¼″ × 6½″ (Unit B). You need a total of 112 Unit B pieces to make the quilt as shown.

**Cut from cream solid:**
- 14 strips 6½″ × 40″

Subcut each strip into 8 rectangles 4¾″ × 6½″ (Unit A). You need a total of 112 Unit A pieces to make the quilt as shown.

**Cut from gray solid:**
- 19 strips 6½″ × 40″

Subcut each strip into 6 squares 6½″ × 6½″. You need a total of 113 solid alternate blocks to make the quilt as shown.

## Piecing and Pressing

To make the quilt as shown, you need to make a total of 112 pieced *All the Above* blocks. Refer to Alternate Sizes and Yardage Requirements (page 36) for additional sizes and block requirements.

For each pieced block, join a Unit A to a Unit B. Press the seams open. The raw pieced blocks measure 6½″ × 6½″.

## Quilt Top Construction

**1.** Arrange the pieced blocks alternately with the solid blocks on a design wall or the floor in 15 rows of 15 blocks each. Try to keep the viewer's eye moving constantly around the quilt top by varying the placement of textures and colors in the pieced blocks, keeping the blocks oriented the same way.

**2.** When you find an arrangement you like, sew the blocks together in rows, pressing the seams open as you sew.

**3.** Sew the rows together. Press the seams open.

Quilt assembly diagram

# Finishing

*Refer to Quiltmaking Basics (pages 62–69) for specifics on layering, quilting, and binding the quilt.*

*All the Above* was quilted with a dense, allover swirl pattern. I chose a shell-colored Aurifil thread that is pretty fine when it's quilted and does not distract from the overall design—that is to say, it's not too light on the gray alternate squares and it's not too dark on the cream pieced squares. Finding a balance here was important to me because I did not want to compromise my initial idea of what I wanted this quilt to look like.

*All the Above* has a straight-grain binding. It's attached by machine and then finished by hand.

*All the Above* can easily be made larger or smaller by changing the number of blocks. The chart below suggests several options and their requirements.

## Alternate Sizes and Yardage Requirements

| Quilt size | Block set | Number of pieced blocks | Number of gray solid blocks | Minimum number of print strips | Cream solid | Gray solid | Backing | Batting | Binding |
|---|---|---|---|---|---|---|---|---|---|
| Baby/wall 42″ × 42″ | 7 × 7 | 24 | 25 | 4 strips 2¼″ × 40″ | 3 strips 6½″ × 40″ (or ¾ yard) | 5 strips 6½″ × 42″ (or 1⅛ yards) | 3 yards | 52″ × 52″ | ½ yard |
| Throw 66″ × 66″ | 11 × 11 | 60 | 61 | 10 strips 2¼″ × 40″ | 8 strips 6½″ × 40″ (or 1⅝ yards) | 11 strips 6½″ × 40″ (or 2¼ yards) | 4¼ yards | 76″ × 76″ | ⅝ yard |
| Twin 78″ × 78″ | 13 × 13 | 84 | 85 | 14 strips 2¼″ × 40″ | 11 strips 6½″ × 40″ (or 2¼ yards) | 15 strips 6½″ × 40″ (or 3 yards) | 5 yards (44″ wide) | 88″ × 88″ | ¾ yard |
| King 114″ × 114″ | 19 × 19 | 180 | 181 | 30 strips 2¼″ × 40″ | 23 strips 6½″ × 40″ (or 4⅓ yards) | 31 strips 6½″ × 40″ (or 5⅞ yards) | 10⅓ yards (42″ wide) | 124″ × 124″ | 1 yard |

## Shake It Up!

Change the look of *All the Above* by using one or more of the following options.

Use only pieced blocks and set them alternately, and reverse the direction of alternate rows.

Scale down the size of the block, use only pieced blocks, and set them so that the narrow rectangles are facing each other. The finished block size in this sample is 3½″ × 3½″.

Using only pieced blocks, set them in horizontal rows, creating a straight line of secondary color. In this example, we used blue florals with red for high contrast.

# Cornerstones

*Cornerstones*, machine pieced by Janine Burke, machine quilted by Jeanette Lone

**FINISHED BLOCK SIZE: 7″ × 7″  •  FINISHED QUILT SIZE: 77″ × 91″**

Batiks have been widely available for many years now, but I remember when they were relatively new. They appealed to me, although I wasn't sure how to use them. I bought them, knowing that someday I would figure it out. Now I collect them. Bold, soft, saturated, muted—I love them all. Over the years of collecting, I've noticed trends in my buying tendencies, and one of them is that I am drawn to the gray-based prints. The whole color spectrum is an open design field for adding gray. *Cornerstones* is made of about 70 different gray-based batiks from my collection. The more, the better!

## MATERIALS

*The yardage given here makes a twin-size quilt. Refer to Alternate Sizes and Yardage Requirements (page 40) for other sizes and yardage requirements.*

**Assorted batiks:** 48 strips 7″ × 40″ or 9⅝ yards total (Each 7″ strip yields enough pieces for 3 *Cornerstones* blocks. You need 143 blocks to make the quilt as shown.)

**Backing:** 5⅝ yards (44″ wide)

**Batting:** 87″ × 101″

**Binding:** ⅞ yard

 **TIP** We usually prewash our batik fabrics to get rid of any residue that may be left over from the production process. We have found that this step makes quilting the top a lot more pleasant.

## CUTTING

**Cut from each 7″ strip:**

• 1 rectangle 7″ × 9″

  Subcut into 1 rectangle 6″ × 9″ (Unit A) and 1 rectangle 1″ × 9″ (Unit B).

• 1 rectangle 7″ × 9″

  Subcut into 1 rectangle 5″ × 9″ (Unit C) and 1 rectangle 2″ × 9″ (Unit D).

• 3 squares 5½″ × 5½″ (Unit E)

## Piecing and Pressing

Each *Cornerstones* block is constructed of 2 contrasting prints: Units A and C from one fabric and Units B, D, and E from the other fabric.

**1.** Sew Units A and D together. Press the seams open. Cut each A/D unit into 6 rectangles 1½″ × 7½″.

**2.** Sew Units B and C together. Press the seams open. Cut each B/C unit into 6 rectangles 1½″ × 5½″.

**3.** Sew a B/C unit to either side of Unit E. Press the seams open.

**4.** Sew an A/D unit to the top and bottom of a B/C/E unit. Press the seams open.

**5.** Make 143 blocks.

## Quilt Top Construction

**1.** Arrange the blocks on a design space such as the floor or a wall. Balance color and texture throughout.

**2.** When you find an arrangement you like, sew the blocks together into rows, pressing seams open as you go.

**3.** Sew the rows together. Press the seams open.

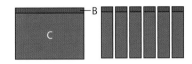

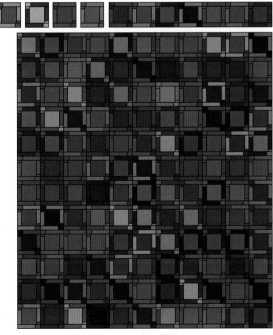

Quilt assembly diagram

# Finishing

*Refer to Quiltmaking Basics (pages 62–69) for specifics on layering, quilting, and binding the quilt.*

*Cornerstones* was quilted with an allover design that adds a lot of curvy texture. The neutral gray thread all but disappears into the fabrics so as not to detract from the fabulous look of all those batiks.

*Cornerstones* has a straight-grain binding, attached by machine and finished by hand.

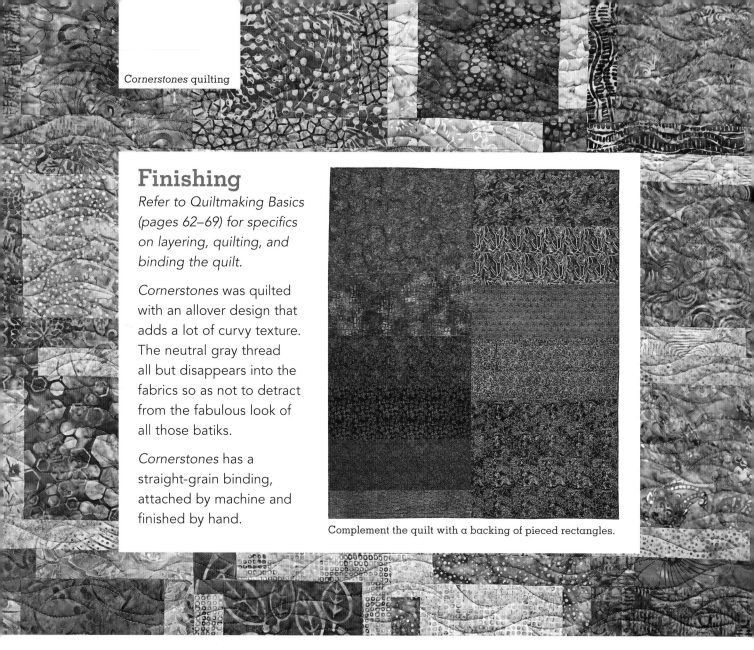

Complement the quilt with a backing of pieced rectangles.

## Alternate Sizes and Yardage Requirements

| Quilt size | Block setting | Number of blocks | Number of 7″ strips | Backing | Batting | Binding |
|---|---|---|---|---|---|---|
| Baby/wall 35″ × 35″ | 5 × 5 | 25 | 9 | 1¼ yards (45″ wide)* | 45″ × 45″ | ³⁄₈ yard |
| Lap/throw 56″ × 63″ | 8 × 9 | 72 | 24 | 3²⁄₃ yards | 66″ × 73″ | ⁵⁄₈ yard |
| Queen 98″ × 105″ | 15 × 14 | 210 | 70 | 9 yards | 108″ × 115″ | 1 yard |

*\* It's okay if the backing is a little smaller than the batting if you can't find 45″-wide fabric.*

# Shake It Up!

Change the look of *Cornerstones* by using one or more of the following options.

Use an analogous color scheme and straight-set blocks with alternating squares.

Set blocks on point.

Set blocks on point and use alternate unpieced squares.

# Sky Blue

*Sky Blue*, machine pieced by Amy Walsh, machine quilted by Ann Davidson

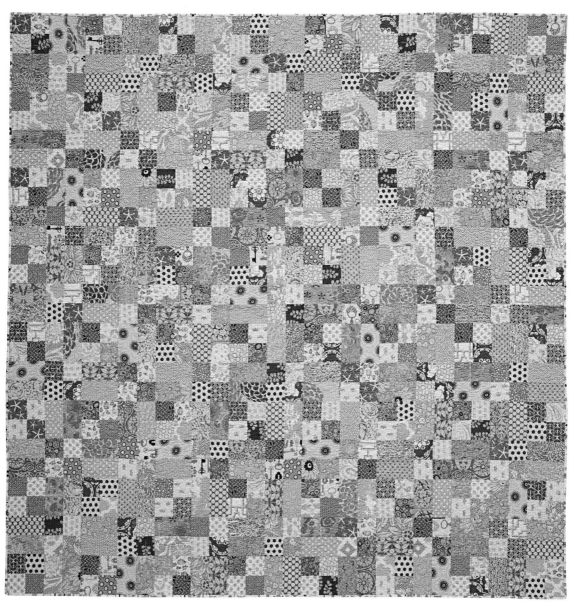

**FINISHED BLOCK SIZE: 5″ × 5″** • **FINISHED QUILT SIZE: 75″ × 75″**

I can remember spending countless hours as a little girl lying in my backyard gazing up at the sky. My grandmother had taught me to look for shapes in the clouds, and I was always amazed at what I could find up there! This quilt started with a collection of soft teals. The decision to add gray and cream came after I realized how the blues reminded me of the beautiful clear skies full of silvery white clouds that were so friendly to me when I was little.

## MATERIALS

*The yardage given here makes a twin-size quilt. Refer to Alternate Sizes and Yardage Requirements (page 45) for other sizes and yardage requirements. A fat quarter is assumed to be 17½″ × 20″.*

*Note:* As always, the more prints, the more interest your quilt will have. I used about 40 prints in this quilt.

Assorted light blue/teal prints: 38 strips 3″ × 40″ (or use 16 fat quarters or 3¼ yards)

Assorted gray prints: 19 strips 3″ × 40″ (or use 8 fat quarters or 1⅔ yards)

Assorted cream/gray and cream/blue prints: 19 strips 3″ × 40″ (or use 8 fat quarters or 1⅔ yards)

Backing: 4¾ yards (43″ wide)

Batting: 85″ × 85″

Binding: ¾ yard

## CUTTING

**Cut from assorted light blue/teal prints:**
• 38 strips 3″ × 40″

Subcut each strip in half to yield 76 strips 3″ × 20″. (If you are using fat quarters, cut each fat quarter into 5 strips 3″ × 20″ for a total of 80 strips. You will have a couple strips left over.)

**Cut from assorted gray prints:**
• 19 strips 3″ × 40″

Subcut each strip in half to yield 38 strips 3″ × 20″. (If you are using fat quarters, cut a total of 38 strips 3″ × 20″.)

**Cut from assorted cream/gray and cream/blue prints:**
• 19 strips 3″ × 40″

Subcut each strip in half to yield 38 strips 3″ × 20″. (If you are using fat quarters, cut a total of 38 strips 3″ × 20″.)

> **TIP** Consider cutting extra strips out of the teal, gray, and cream to make more blocks than called for. This way you have more color options when arranging the blocks for the quilt top.

## Piecing and Pressing

*Sky Blue* is made with 2 alternating blocks: cream and gray Four-Patches and teal double rectangle blocks. To make the quilt as shown, you need 113 Four-Patch blocks and 112 double rectangle blocks. See Alternate Sizes and Yardage Requirements (page 45) for additional sizes and block requirements.

### Four-Patch Block Construction

**1.** Sew a cream strip to a gray strip. Press the seams open. The raw unit measures 5½″ × 20″. Make a total of 38.

**2.** Cut each strip set from Step 1 into 6 units 3″ × 5½″.

**3.** Sew 2 cream / gray units from Step 2 together. Press the seams open. The raw Four-Patch blocks measure 5½″ × 5½″. Repeat to make 113 blocks.

## Double Rectangle Block Construction

**1.** Sew a set of 2 teal / light blue 3″ × 20″ strips together to make the double rectangle strata. Press the seams open. The raw strata measures 5½″ × 20″. Repeat to make 38 strata.

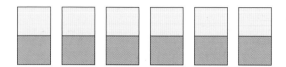

**2.** Subcut a strata unit from Step 1 into 3 squares 5½″ × 5½″. Repeat to cut 112 squares.

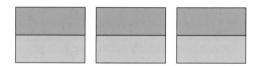

## Quilt Top Construction

**1.** Arrange the blocks alternately in 15 rows of 15 blocks each, using the quilt assembly diagram as needed.

**2.** When you find an arrangement that you like, sew the blocks together into rows, pressing the seams open as you sew.

**3.** Sew the rows together. Press the seams open.

Quilt assembly diagram

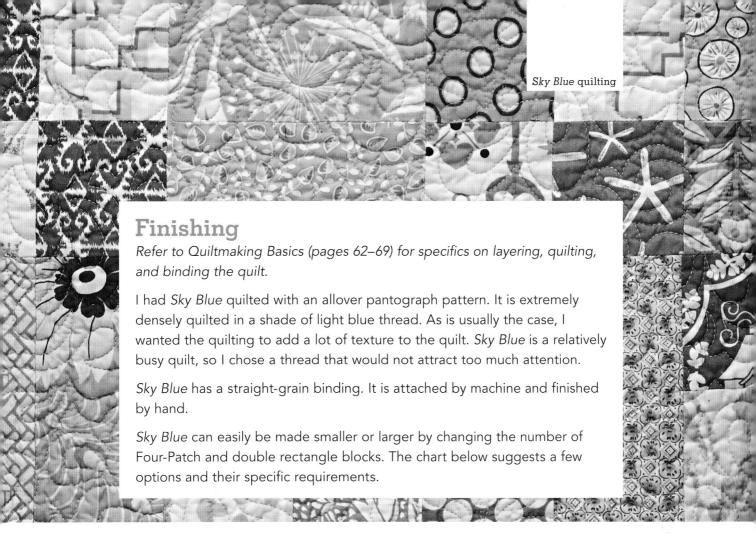

*Sky Blue* quilting

# Finishing

*Refer to Quiltmaking Basics (pages 62–69) for specifics on layering, quilting, and binding the quilt.*

I had *Sky Blue* quilted with an allover pantograph pattern. It is extremely densely quilted in a shade of light blue thread. As is usually the case, I wanted the quilting to add a lot of texture to the quilt. *Sky Blue* is a relatively busy quilt, so I chose a thread that would not attract too much attention.

*Sky Blue* has a straight-grain binding. It is attached by machine and finished by hand.

*Sky Blue* can easily be made smaller or larger by changing the number of Four-Patch and double rectangle blocks. The chart below suggests a few options and their specific requirements.

### Alternate Sizes and Yardage Requirements

| Quilt size | Block set | Number of Four-Patch blocks | Number of double rectangle blocks | Number of gray and cream print strips (3″ × 20″) | Number of light blue/teal strips (3″ × 20″) | Backing | Batting | Binding |
|---|---|---|---|---|---|---|---|---|
| Baby/wall 35″ × 35″ | 7 × 7 | 25 | 24 | 9 gray, 9 cream | 16 | 2½ yards **or** 1¼ yards (45″ wide) | 45″ × 45″ | ⅜ yard |
| Throw 55″ × 55″ | 11 × 11 | 61 | 60 | 21 gray, 21 cream | 40 | 3⅝ yards | 65″ × 65″ | ⅝ yard |
| Queen 95″ × 95″ | 19 × 19 | 181 | 180 | 61 gray, 61 cream | 120 | 8¾ yards | 105″ × 105″ | ⅞ yard |
| King 115″ × 115″ | 23 × 23 | 265 | 264 | 89 gray, 89 cream | 176 | 10½ yards (42″ wide) | 125″ × 125″ | 1 yard |

## Shake It Up!

You can drastically change the look of *Sky Blue* by using one or more of the following options.

With solids, use a monochromatic or analogous palette for both the Four-Patch and the double rectangle blocks. Choose colors that are high contrast for the greatest impact.

Make complete blocks using sets of four double rectangle and Four-Patch blocks. Alternate the completed blocks. We've also changed the color scheme for this example, opting for reds and pinks in place of the blues and teals.

Set the Four-Patch blocks and double rectangle blocks in alternate columns. I think this setting would make a great "guy quilt" with the right color palette.

# Around Town

*Around Town*, machine pieced by Janine Burke, machine quilted by Ann Davidson

**FINISHED BLOCK SIZE:** 6″ × 10″ • **FINISHED QUILT SIZE:** 66″ × 80″

Amy and I frequently comment that it's all about the fabric. We love fabric. Whether it's saturated or muted, solid or textured, we love working with it. I thought the essence of this quilt would best be captured in the fabulous fabric collections by Marcia Derse. I really enjoyed incorporating many of her prints into this one project. If you haven't had the chance to work with her fabrics, we would encourage you to do so. Not only do they play well together from one collection to another, but they look fabulous.

## MATERIALS

*The yardage given here makes a twin-size quilt. Refer to Alternate Sizes and Yardage Requirements (page 49) for other sizes and yardage requirements.*

**Assorted contrasting prints:**
30 strips 7½″ × 40″
or 6½ yards total

**Backing:** 5 yards

**Binding:** ⅝ yard

**Batting:** 76″ × 90″

## CUTTING

**From assorted contrasting print strips:**

• Cut each 7½″ × 40″ strip into 3 strips 2½″ × 40″.

Subcut each 2½″ × 40″ strip into:

3 rectangles 2½″ × 6½″ (Unit A)

4 rectangles 2½″ × 2″ (Unit B)

6 rectangles 2½″ × 1½″ (Unit C)

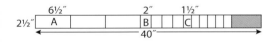

# Piecing and Pressing

To make the sample quilt, you need to make a total of 80 complete blocks and 8 partial blocks (a complete block separated into components that are placed at the top and bottom of a column). Refer to Alternate Sizes and Yardage Requirements (page 49) for additional sizes and block requirements.

Each *Around Town* block uses 3 Unit A pieces, 4 Unit B pieces, and 2 Unit C pieces from a single print and 4 Unit C pieces from a contrasting print.

**1.** Sew 2 Unit B and 3 Unit C rectangles together as shown. Press the seams open. Make 2 using the same print combinations.

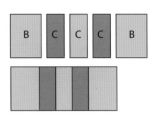

**2.** Sew the 2 B/C units from Step 1 together with 3 Unit A rectangles. Press the seams open. The raw block measures 6½″ × 10½″.

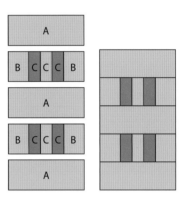

**3.** Repeat Steps 1 and 2 to make 80 complete blocks.

**4.** See the quilt assembly diagram (page 49) as needed and make 8 partial blocks. Partial blocks are constructed in the same manner as a complete block except that they are split into 2 sections. For example, columns 2 and 7 have a Unit A rectangle at the top, with the remainder of the block at the bottom, and columns 5 and 10 have the placement reversed. Columns 3 and 8 have a B/C unit and a Unit A rectangle at the top, with the remainder of the block at the bottom, and columns 4 and 9 have the placement reversed.

**TIP** A precise ¼″ seam is important for this block to ensure an accurate fit. If you find that the B/C units are longer or shorter than Unit A, your machine's seams are too small or too large, respectively, and you must adjust accordingly.

## Quilt Top Construction

**1.** Arrange the blocks and partial blocks into 11 columns, balancing the color and texture to ensure that the viewer's eye moves smoothly across the quilt top.

**2.** When you have arranged the blocks, sew them together, pressing the seams open. Note that columns 2–5 and 7–10 are offset by the partial blocks.

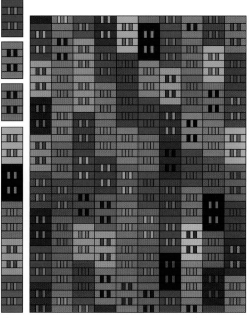

Quilt assembly diagram—for block placement and a guide for balancing color

## Finishing

*Refer to Quiltmaking Basics (pages 62–69) for specifics on layering, quilting, and binding the quilt.*

*Around Town* was quilted with an allover design in a neutral green thread so as not to distract from the fabrics. This quilt is all about the fabrics! It has a straight-grain binding, attached by machine and finished by hand.

### Alternate Sizes and Yardage Requirements

| Quilt Size | Block setting | Number of blocks | Number of 2½″ strips | Backing | Batting | Binding |
|---|---|---|---|---|---|---|
| Baby/wall 36″ × 40″ | 6 × 4 | 24 | 24 | 1⅜ yards (44″ wide)* | 46″ × 50″ | ½ yard |
| Throw/lap 48″ × 50″ | 8 × 5 | 40 | 40 | 3¼ yards | 58″ × 60″ | ½ yard |
| Queen 96″ × 100″ | 16 × 10 | 160 | 160 | 9 yards | 106″ × 110″ | ⅞ yard |
| King 120″ × 120″ | 20 × 12 | 240 | 240 | 10⅞ yards (44″ wide) | 130″ × 130″ | 1 yard |

*\* Backing is slightly smaller than batting.*

# Shake It Up!

Change the look of *Around Town* by changing the block setting.

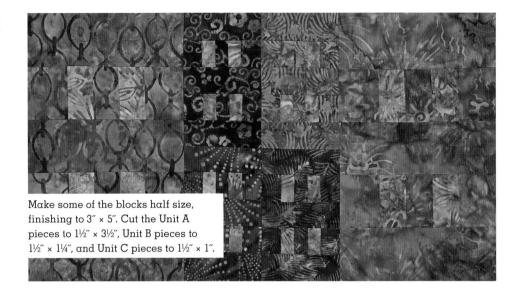

Make some of the blocks half size, finishing to 3″ × 5″. Cut the Unit A pieces to 1½″ × 3½″, Unit B pieces to 1½″ × 1¼″, and Unit C pieces to 1½″ × 1″.

If you don't want to make partial blocks, you can set the blocks in straight rows and columns instead of offsetting them.

Use the straight setting and add alternating nonpieced blocks. We used batiks for this one.

# Balcony Seating

*Balcony Seating*, machine pieced by Janine Burke, machine quilted by Ann Davidson

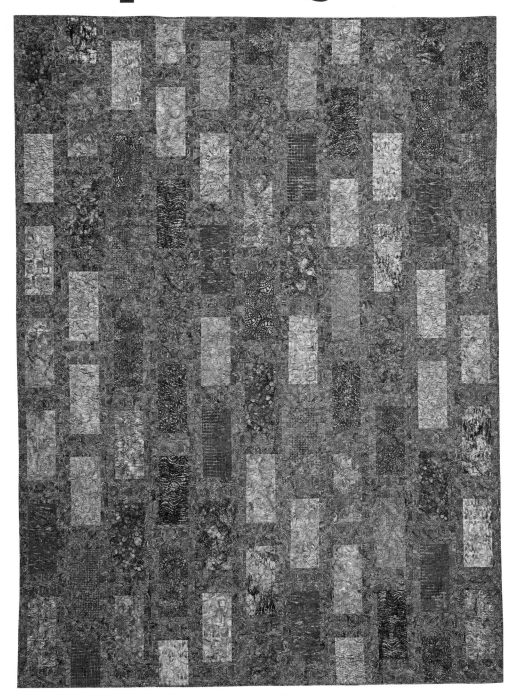

**FINISHED BLOCK SIZE: 6˝ × 9˝** • **FINISHED QUILT SIZE: 66˝ × 87˝**

Whether I'm in the theater or watching a scene produced in a theater, the privacy of the balconies appeals to me. Spots of color are visible in the semidarkness, hinting at the gowns and apparel worn by the theatergoers. The muted palette I chose for *Balcony Seating* hints at the intimate setting of theaters, then and now.

## MATERIALS

*The yardage given here makes a twin-size quilt. Refer to Alternate Sizes and Yardage Requirements (page 53) for other sizes and yardage requirements.*

**Assorted colorful batiks:** 21 strips 4½″ × 40″ or 2¾ yards total

**Gray batik:** 3⅜ yards

**Backing:** 5½ yards

**Batting:** 76″ × 97″

**Binding:** ¾ yard

 We usually prewash our batik fabrics to get rid of any residue that may be left over from the production process. We have found that this step makes quilting the top a lot more pleasant.

## CUTTING

**Cut from colorful batik:**
• 21 strips 4½″ × 40″

**Cut from gray batik:**
• 8 strips 6½″ × 40″

  Subcut each strip into 11 rectangles 3½″ × 6½″ (used as spacers).

• 42 strips 1½″ × 40″

# Piecing and Pressing

The blocks for *Balcony Seating* are constructed by making strata, or strip-pieced units. You make a total of 21 strata, from the 21 assorted colorful batik 4½″ × 40″ strips combined with gray batik strips. Each strata unit yields 4 blocks.

**1.** Sew a gray 1½″ × 40″ strip to either long side of a 4½″ × 40″ strip. Press the seams open. Repeat to make 21 strata.

**2.** Cut each strata unit into 4 rectangles 6½″ × 9½″ to make 82 blocks. There are 2 extra.

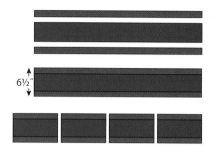

**NOTE**  Of the 82 pieced blocks required to complete this quilt, 10 become partial blocks. Cut these 10 blocks into 6½″ × 6½″ squares to be set at the top and bottom of the even-numbered columns. Refer to Quilt Top Construction.

# Quilt Top Construction

**1.** Refer to the quilt assembly diagram as necessary to place the blocks and gray spacers into columns. Note that the odd-numbered columns (1, 3, 5, 7, 9, and 11) have a gray spacer at the top and bottom, whereas the even-numbered columns (2, 4, 6, 8, and 10) have a partial block on the top and bottom. As you arrange the blocks, balance the colors throughout so that the viewer's eye moves smoothly over the quilt top.

**2.** When you've found an arrangement you like, sew the blocks and spacers into columns, pressing the seams open.

**3.** Sew the columns together, pressing the seams open.

Quilt assembly diagram

In Love with Squares & Rectangles

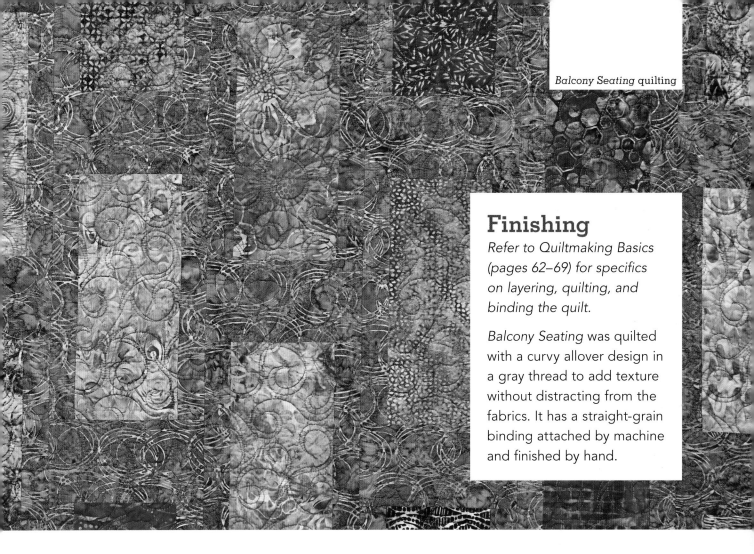

# Finishing

*Refer to Quiltmaking Basics (pages 62–69) for specifics on layering, quilting, and binding the quilt.*

*Balcony Seating* was quilted with a curvy allover design in a gray thread to add texture without distracting from the fabrics. It has a straight-grain binding attached by machine and finished by hand.

## Alternate Sizes and Yardage Requirements

| Quilt size | Number of columns | Number of pieced blocks* | Number of 4½″ strips | Number of gray spacers | Gray yardage | Backing | Batting | Binding |
|---|---|---|---|---|---|---|---|---|
| Baby/wall 30″ × 39″ | 5 | 17 | 5 | 18 | 1 yard cut into 2 strips 6½″ × 40″ and 10 strips 1½″ × 40″ | 1⅜ yards | 40″ × 49″ | ⅜ yard |
| Lap/throw 54″ × 63″ | 9 | 49 | 13 | 50 | 2¼ yards cut into 5 strips 6½″ × 40″ and 26 strips 1½″ × 40″ | 3⅝ yards | 64″ × 73″ | ⅝ yard |
| Queen 87″ × 102″ | 17 | 127 | 32 | 128 | 5⅛ yards cut into 12 strips 6½″ × 40″ and 64 strips 1½″ × 40″ | 8⅛ yards | 97″ × 112″ | ⅞ yard |
| King 114″ × 123″ | 19 | 199 | 50 | 200 | 7⅞ yards cut into 19 strips 6½″ × 40″ and 100 strips 1½″ × 40″ | 11⅛ yards (42″ wide) | 124″ × 133″ | 1 yard |

*This number includes partial blocks.*

## Shake It Up!

Change the look of *Balcony Seating* by using one or more of the following options.

Use bold prints and cut the "balconies" to finish at 5″ × 10″ with 2″ finished separators, for a smaller, more compact "theater."

Use large-scale prints and cut the balconies to finish at 6″ × 6″ with 2″ finished separators.

Using large-scale prints, cut the balconies to finish at 4″ × 4″ with 2″ finished black separators. Notice how framing the squares in black really adds to the drama.

# Square Dance

*Square Dance*, machine pieced by Amy Walsh, machine quilted by Ann Davidson

**FINISHED BLOCK SIZE: 9″ × 14″ • FINISHED QUILT SIZE: 54″ × 70″**

At some point after I started quilting, I made my first Log Cabin quilt. Ever since then, I have wanted to make some wonky Log Cabin quilts. *Square Dance* is the first of these designs. The colors in this quilt make the design lines very apparent. Try using a more analogous palette for a more subtle look, or make the quilt out of some nonsolid fabrics (refer to photos of different looks on pages 60 and 61). Batiks or modern-looking fabrics, such as Marcia Derse's prints, would be perfect here.

# MATERIALS

*The yardage given here makes a throw-size quilt. Refer to Alternate Sizes and Yardage Requirements (page 59) for other sizes and yardage requirements.*

**Quilt top:** 30 fat quarters in assorted bright solid colors

(We used Robert Kaufman Kona Cotton Solids and Cherrywood Fabrics solids in the following colors: red, white, cobalt blue, teal blue, lime green, yellow-green, kelly green, canary yellow, orange, yellow-orange, fuchsia, purple, and lavender. Note that with 30 fat quarters you will have leftover fabric when you have finished the quilt top. However, you will also have enough to allow for any cutting errors you may make and changes in color choices as you are sewing.)

**Backing:** 3⅝ yards

**Batting:** 64″ × 80″

**Binding:** ½ yard

# CUTTING

*Square Dance* is made with 3 different blocks: A, B, and C. You can customize the look of the quilt by changing the number of A, B, and C blocks that you use. The featured quilt uses 11 of Block A, 8 of Block B, and 11 of Block C.

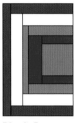  

Block A          Block B          Block C

Before you begin cutting, decide how many of each block you would like to make, keeping in mind that you will need 30 blocks total to make the quilt as shown. Then cut the pieces for each block using the cutting information in the chart below, varying the colors for each concentric partial loop as you like. The loops of each block are differentiated with highlights in the following chart.

## Cut Sizes

| Block A | Block B | Block C |
|---|---|---|
| 1 square 4½″ × 4½″ | 1 rectangle 3½″ × 4″ | 1 rectangle 6″ × 5½″ |
| 2 rectangles 1½″ × 4½″<br>1 rectangle 2¼″ × 6½″ | 2 rectangles 1½″ × 4″<br>1 rectangle 1½″ × 5½″ | 2 rectangles 2¼″ × 5½″<br>1 rectangle 1¾″ × 9½″ |
| 2 rectangles 1¾″ × 6¼″<br>1 rectangle 1¼″ × 9″ | 2 rectangles 2″ × 5″<br>1 rectangle 2″ × 8½″ | 2 rectangles 2″ × 6¾″<br>1 rectangle 1¾″ × 12½″ |
| 2 rectangles 2″ × 7″<br>1 rectangle 2″ × 12″ | 2 rectangles 1¾″ × 6½″<br>1 rectangle 2½″ × 11″ | 2 rectangles 1½″ × 8″<br>1 rectangle 2″ × 14½″ |
| 2 rectangles 1¾″ × 8½″<br>1 rectangle 1½″ × 14½″ | 2 rectangles 2¼″ × 8½″<br>1 rectangle 1½″ × 14½″ | |

 **TIP** I usually prefer to do most of the cutting for a quilt at one time for the sake of efficiency. However, when cutting *Square Dance*, I cut out each block separately, making the color choices as I went along. This way, I could ensure that I had enough contrast within each block to make the design apparent. I could also better control the amount of each color I was using throughout the entire quilt.

*In Love with Squares & Rectangles*

# Piecing and Pressing

Each of the 3 *Square Dance* blocks is constructed the same way, by starting with the center unit and adding the top and bottom units, pressing the seams open after each addition. The following instructions are for Block A. Apply the same methods when constructing Blocks B and C.

**1.** Sew 2 rectangles 1½˝ × 4½˝ to the top and bottom of the center 4½˝ × 4½˝ square. Press the seams open.

**2.** Sew 1 rectangle 2¼˝ × 6½˝ to the side of the unit. Press the seam open.

**3.** Sew 2 rectangles 1¾˝ × 6¼˝ to the top and bottom of the unit. Press the seams open.

**4.** Sew 1 rectangle 1¼˝ × 9˝ to the side of the unit. Press the seam open.

**5.** Sew 2 rectangles 2˝ × 7˝ to the top and bottom of the unit. Press the seams open.

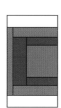

**6.** Sew 1 rectangle 2˝ × 12˝ to the side of the unit. Press the seam open.

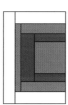

**7.** Sew 2 rectangles 1¾˝ × 8½˝ to the top and bottom of the unit. Press the seams open.

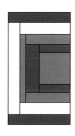

**8.** Sew the remaining 1½˝ × 14½˝ rectangle to the side of the unit. Press the seam open. The raw block measures 9½˝ × 14½˝.

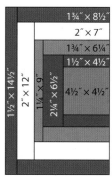

Block A, cut sizes shown

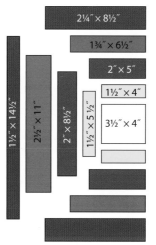

Block B, cut sizes shown

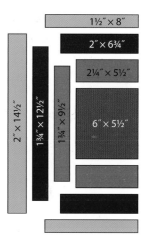

Block C, cut sizes shown

> **TIP** An accurate ¼˝ seam is essential to sewing the *Square Dance* blocks together. If your machine's seams are inaccurate, you will find that the pieces you are adding are either too short (if the seams are too narrow) or too long (if the seams are too wide). Before you begin sewing, be sure to test the accuracy of your machine's seams and adjust accordingly.

# Quilt Top Construction

**1.** When you have completed 30 *Square Dance* blocks, arrange them on a design wall or the floor into 5 rows of 6 blocks each, dispersing colors and different blocks evenly throughout the quilt, and alternating block orientations as shown.

**2.** When you find an arrangement that you like, sew the blocks together in rows, pressing the seams open as you sew.

**3.** Sew the rows together, pressing the seams open.

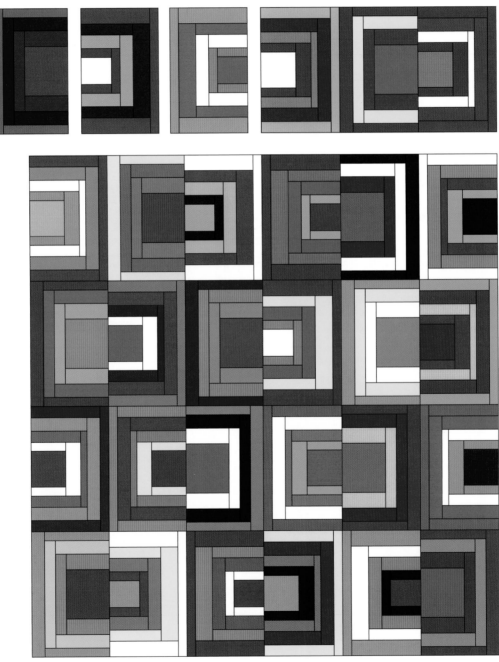

Quilt assembly diagram

# Finishing

*Refer to Quiltmaking Basics (pages 62–69) for specifics on layering, quilting, and binding the quilt.*

*Square Dance* is densely quilted with an allover pattern called Banana Swirl Pantograph by Barbara Becker. I chose white Aurifil thread—it does not show up on the white fabrics at all, and because it is so fine, it does not overpower the bright solids. When confronted with a thread decision in a quilt that includes dark and light fabrics, I almost always opt for a thread that matches the lighter fabrics. This is the more traditional option. However, a dark thread, such as red or teal, would have caused the white solid in this quilt to appear less stark, which would lessen the contrast between the whites and the bright colors.

*Square Dance* has a straight-grain binding. It is attached by machine and finished by hand.

*Square Dance* can easily be made larger or smaller by altering the number of blocks. The chart below suggests some sizes and their yardage requirements.

### Alternate Sizes and Yardage Requirements

| Quilt size | Number of blocks | Block set | Number of assorted fat quarters | Backing | Batting | Binding |
|---|---|---|---|---|---|---|
| Baby/wall 36″ × 42″ | 12 | 4 × 3 | 12 | 1½ yards (44″ wide)* | 46″ × 52″ | ½ yard |
| Twin 72″ × 98″ | 56 | 8 × 7 | 56 | 6 yards (41″ wide) | 82″ × 108″ | ⅞ yard |
| Queen 90″ × 112″ | 80 | 10 × 8 | 80 | 8⅓ yards (41″ wide) | 100″ × 122″ | 1 yard |
| King 108″ × 126″ | 108 | 12 × 9 | 108 | 11⅓ yards | 118″ × 136″ | 1 yard |

*\* It is okay if the backing is a little smaller than the batting.*
*Note: As with the sample quilt, the required yardage for the above quilts will leave extra fabric.*

# Shake It Up!

You can change the look of *Square Dance* by using one or more of the following options.

Use only one block type and set pairs of the blocks facing each other to make a rectangular Log Cabin–type pattern. Here, we've used modern prints with white for a fresh, airy feeling.

For a funkier-looking quilt, try offsetting the blocks as in this example, made out of bright batiks.

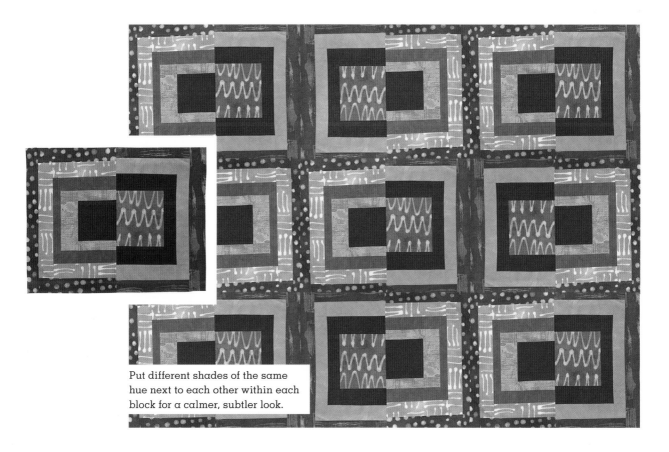

Put different shades of the same hue next to each other within each block for a calmer, subtler look.

# Quiltmaking Basics

## Our Favorite Tools

Although we would argue that if you *really* want to sew, you can do so with a minimum of fuss and special gadgets, we have found that some tools are indispensible in our studios. We have listed them here. They are widely available and not very expensive, and having them close at hand when you go to sew makes life *so* much easier.

## Rotary Cutters

A good rotary cutter is a must in any quilter's studio. We prefer the Olfa brand with the 60mm blades. It cuts through multiple layers easily and seems to be the most comfortable to hold for both of us. Don't skimp on the blades! We have heard many of our students remark that they do not like to change the blade because of the expense. If you are willing to spend $11 per yard on fabric, then be willing to change your blade to save yourself wrist strain and discomfort. A sharper blade will also yield more accurate cuts and less stress (always a benefit to us).

## Rulers

If you are new to quilting, find a set of rulers that appeal to you. Don't be afraid to try different brands until you find your favorite. At Blue Underground Studios, we tend to favor the Omnigrip rulers, and we each have a set of 14″ and 24″ to work with. Amy also favors the Trudie Hughes rulers marketed through Patched Works, Inc., in Elm Grove, Wisconsin. Her favorites are the Big Mama and Big Daddy rulers.

Finding a ruler you like to work with will help you to cut more accurately and reduce stress when you start a project. Are you seeing a theme here? We are all about reducing the stress in quilting!

## Superfine Glass-Head Pins

We prefer the pins with a 0.50mm steel shaft. The shaft on these pins is fine enough to reduce bulk in seams that we are pinning together. This allows us to sew all the way up to the matched seams, reducing slipping so that all the corners are perfect!

## General's Chalk Pencils

We love to have these pencils on hand to mark our blocks as we are sewing quilt tops together. The lighter colors (white, gray, or light blue) adhere to the fabrics long enough for us to sew the entire quilt top together and then disappear completely in the wash.

| TIP | Stay away from dark colors on white/light fabrics. They may not wash out. |
|---|---|

## Thread

Great thread is another must in a quilting studio. We like to use a fine thread, such as Aurifil. It works beautifully with cotton fabrics, bobbins can hold a ton of it, and it also makes a great quilting thread. As a general rule, we like to piece with a neutral thread such as gray or tan. However, we make our thread decisions on a case-by-case basis. Sometimes the fabric we are piecing begs for matching thread, especially when we are pressing seams open.

In Love with Squares & Rectangles

# Fabric

Quilters have a wide variety of fabrics available from many different sources. Don't skimp on fabric—treat yourself and buy the best. There is a real value in building a good stash of quality fabric. First of all, trends in fabric change all the time. Colors and styles are constantly evolving. So when you find a print you love, don't be afraid to buy it. We often add fabrics from our stashes to new collections we have purchased.

## Prewashing Fabric

Prewashing fabric is a matter of personal preference in most cases. We usually don't prewash our cotton prints simply because of the time it takes, but we always wash batiks because of the wax used in the production process. Sometimes this residue can build up on a needle during sewing or quilting, leading to tension problems. We have found that laundered batiks are almost always easier to work with. We also wash most of the solids that we work with to ensure that they are colorfast. We recommend washing solids with Retayne, a chemical fixative for commercial fabrics. You can use Retayne for any commercial fabrics you work with, especially if you are worried about the colors running onto one another.

# Seam Allowances

A ¼″ seam allowance is used for all of the projects in this book. It's a good idea to do a test seam before you begin sewing to check that your ¼″ is accurate. Accuracy is the key to successful piecing. There is no need to backstitch. Seamlines will be crossed by another seam, which will anchor them.

**TIP** Not sure about your ¼″ seam? Try this simple exercise.

- Using scraps, cut 3 rectangles that measure 1½″ × 3″.

- Sew the rectangles together and press the seams open.

- If the unit measures *exactly* 3½″ wide, you have a "perfect" ¼″ seam allowance. Keep in mind that this may vary by a thread width from project to project, depending on the fabrics you are using.

- If the unit measures *less than* 3½″ wide, the seams are too big. It may be just a thread width or two, but it will make a difference, so the seams should be adjusted accordingly.

- If the unit measures *more than* 3½″ wide, the seams are too small. Again, it may be just a thread width or two, but the seams should be adjusted accordingly.

Repeat this exercise until you are satisfied with your ¼″ seam allowance.

# Pressing

We prefer to press all of our seams open! If you have not tried this before, give it a shot. We love the flat, graphic nature of quilts that have absolutely flat seams. Press lightly in an up-and-down motion. Avoid using an overly hot iron or over-ironing, which can distort shapes and blocks. We do like to use steam as well.

*Note:* The only time ironing seams open is not appropriate is if you are planning to hand quilt your top. Machine quilting will anchor flat-pressed seams, making them stand up to washing and wear.

# Constructing a Quilt Top

## Borders

Adding a border to a quilt is a distinct design decision. We usually prefer to make quilts without borders for a couple reasons. Quilts tend to be more interesting if you make more blocks to increase their size rather than just add a border. In addition, if you use a printed border fabric, you may run the risk of your quilt looking out of date. (*Note:* This is usually not the case for quilts with solid borders.) Remember that fabric trends come and go as easily as clothing trends.

When we do add a border to a quilt, we prefer to cut the pieces parallel to the selvage using long pieces of fabric to avoid piecing them together. However, piecing works fine when you do not have enough length of fabric.

### BUTTED BORDERS

In most cases the side borders are sewn on first. When you have finished the quilt top, measure it vertically through the center. This is the length to cut the side borders. Place pins at the center of all four edges of the quilt top, as well as in the center of each side border strip. Pin the side borders to the quilt top first, matching the center pins. Using a ¼˝ seam allowance, sew the borders to the quilt top and press the seam open.

Measure horizontally across the center of the quilt top, including the side borders. This is the length to cut the top and bottom borders. Repeat pinning, sewing, and pressing.

# Finishing

We recommend that you give careful consideration to all of the finishing elements of a quilt. Careful choices for batting, backing, quilting, and binding can make a good quilt top into a spectacular quilt. Likewise, poor choices can undermine your hard work and money!

## Backing

Plan on making the backing a minimum of 10˝ longer and wider than the quilt top. For all of the larger quilts in this book, you will need to piece the backing from multiple yardage lengths. Specific yardage requirements are given for each quilt. If you are sending your quilt top to a longarm quilter to be finished, be sure you check to see if the quilter has any requirements for the backing. Most quilters want extra fabric on all sides of the backing as well as a squared back so that they can begin working on your quilt with minimal trouble.

If you have time, consider piecing the back from any leftover quilting fabrics or blocks in your collection. This not only can save you money and make more room in your stash for new fabric, but it also gives you the chance to customize the look of your back. Try adding fabrics that mean something to you or the recipient of the quilt. And add a label. These little details can add so much to your finished project.

## Batting

Consider your batting choices carefully. Many batting choices are available today. Since we wash almost all of our quilts after they are bound, we choose battings that will not only stand up to multiple washings but also give an antiqued look after they are laundered. Our favorite batts are Hobbs Heirloom 80/20, Hobbs Heirloom Wool, and Quilters Dream Select Loft. Each of these batts is thin enough to use for a wallhanging and has enough drape to use in a full- or queen-size quilt.

## Layering

If you choose to quilt the top yourself and do not have a longarm, you will need to layer and baste the quilt carefully. Spread the backing wrong side up and tape the edges down with masking tape. (If you are working on carpet you can use T-pins to secure the backing to the carpet.) Center the batting on top, smoothing out any folds. Place the quilt top right side up on top of the batting and backing, making sure it is centered.

## Basting

Basting keeps the quilt sandwich layers from shifting while you are quilting.

If you plan to machine quilt, pin baste the quilt layers together with safety pins placed a minimum of 3″–4″ apart. Begin basting in the center and move toward the edges in vertical then horizontal rows. Try not to pin directly on the intended quilting lines.

If you plan to hand quilt, baste the layers together with thread using a long needle and light-colored thread. Knot one end of the thread. Using stitches approximately the length of the needle, begin in the center and move out toward the edges in vertical and horizontal rows approximately 4″ apart. Add two diagonal rows of basting.

## Quilting

Quilting, whether by hand or machine, should enhance the pieced design of the quilt. All the quilts presented here lend themselves well to allover freehand or pantograph patterns. We love the texture that allover quilting produces, especially once a quilt has been laundered. We prefer the look of very densely quilted designs that keep the eye moving across the quilt top. If you like to do your own quilting, try free-motion designs such as spirals, meanders, or paisleys.

If you work with a longarm quilter, take advantage of that person's experience. Professional quilters pair designs with quilt tops for a living. Use your quilter and his or her knowledge as a valuable resource.

Many professional quilters have computer-guided machines that make dense quilting more affordable and accessible.

## Binding

Trim excess batting and backing from the quilt even with the edges of the quilt top and square up the corners.

**DOUBLE-FOLD STRAIGHT-GRAIN BINDING**
If you want a ¼″ finished binding, cut the binding strips 2½″ wide and piece them together with diagonal seams to make a continuous binding strip. Trim the seams to ¼″. Press the seams open. *Binding yardage is given in the projects for 2½″-wide strips with an extra strip in case of a bad cut.* We prefer a thinner binding, so we cut our strips either 2″ or 2¼″ wide.

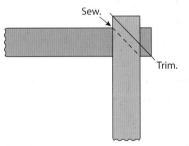

Sew from corner to corner.

Completed diagonal seam

Press the entire strip in half lengthwise with wrong sides together. With raw edges even, pin the binding to the front edge of the quilt a few inches away from a corner, and leave the first few inches of the binding unattached. Start sewing, using a ¼″ seam allowance.

Stop ¼″ away from the first corner (Step 1), and backstitch one stitch. Lift the presser foot and needle. Rotate the quilt one-quarter turn. Fold the binding at a right angle so it extends straight above the quilt and the fold forms a 45° angle in the corner (Step 2). Then bring the binding strip down even with the edge of the quilt (Step 3). Begin sewing at the folded edge. Repeat in the same manner at all corners.

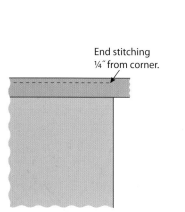
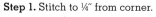
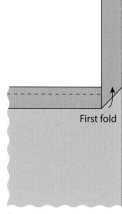
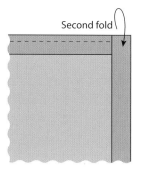

**Step 1.** Stitch to ¼″ from corner.　　**Step 2.** First fold for miter　　**Step 3.** Second fold alignment

Continue stitching until you are back near the beginning of the binding strip. Stop stitching about 6″ before you reach the beginning stitching. See Finishing the Binding Ends (page 69) for tips on finishing and hiding the raw edges of the ends of the binding.

## CONTINUOUS BIAS BINDING

A continuous bias involves using a square sliced in half diagonally and then sewing the resulting triangles together so that you continuously cut marked strips to make continuous bias binding. The same instructions can be used to cut bias for piping. Cut the fabric for the bias binding or piping into a square. For example, if yardage is ½ yard, cut an 18″ × 18″ square. Cut the square in half diagonally, creating 2 triangles.

Sew these triangles together as shown, using a ¼″ seam allowance. Press the seam open.

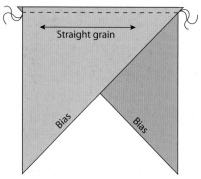

Sew triangles together.

Using a ruler, mark the parallelogram created by the 2 triangles with lines spaced the width you need to cut on the bias. Cut about 5″ along the first line.

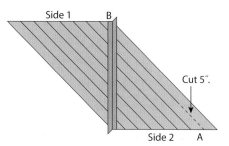

Mark lines and begin cut.

In Love with Squares & Rectangles

Join Side 1 and Side 2 to form a tube. The raw edge at line A will align with the raw edge at B. This will allow the first line to be offset by the width of one strip. Pin the raw edges right sides together, making sure that the lines match. Sew with a ¼˝ seam allowance. Press the seam open. Cut along the drawn lines, creating one continuous strip.

Cut along
drawn line.

Press the entire strip in half lengthwise with wrong sides together. Place binding on quilt as described in Double-Fold Straight-Grain Binding (page 67). See Finishing the Binding Ends (below) for tips on finishing and hiding the raw edges of the ends of the binding.

**FINISHING THE BINDING ENDS**
Method 1
After stitching around the quilt, fold the short end of the beginning tail of the binding strip over ¼˝ so that the raw edge will be inside the binding after it is turned to the back of the quilt. Place the end tail of the binding strip on top of the beginning folded end. Continue to attach the binding, and stitch slightly beyond the starting stitches. Trim the excess binding. Fold the binding over the raw edges to the quilt back and hand stitch, mitering the corners.

Method 2
Fold the ending tail of the binding back on itself where it meets the beginning binding tail. From the fold, measure and mark the cut width of the binding strip. Cut the ending binding tail to this measurement. For example, if the binding is

cut 2½˝ wide, measure 2½˝ from the fold on the ending tail of the binding and cut the binding tail to this length.

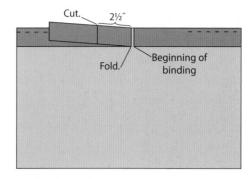

Cut binding tail.

Open both tails. Place one tail on top of the other tail at right angles, right sides together. Mark a diagonal line from corner to corner and stitch on the line. Check that you've done it correctly and that the binding fits the quilt; then trim the seam allowance to ¼˝. Press open.

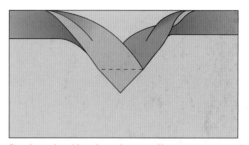

Stitch ends of binding diagonally.

Refold the binding and stitch this binding section in place on the quilt. Fold the binding over the raw edges to the quilt back and hand stitch.

# Laundering Quilts
We launder all of our cotton quilts after they are bound. Laundering gives our quilts the shrinky look that we love in addition to taking out all of the chemicals that may be in the fabrics from the production process. Use a mild quilt soap (never use a regular detergent). Wash quilts on the gentlest cycle possible. We usually dry quilts on the lowest setting and take them out of the dryer before they are completely dry.

# Favorite Resources

## Books and Tools on Color

Barnes, Christine E. *The Quilter's Color Club.* Lafayette, CA: C&T Publishing, 2011.

*A great resource for knowledge of color in quilting! Exercises are very valuable for building confidence.*

Eiseman, Leatrice. *Color: Messages and Meanings.* Gloucester, MA: Hand Books Press, 2006.

*Invaluable resource for exploring each color separately.*

Menz, Deb. *Color Works.* Loveland, CO: Interweave Press, 2004.

*Good resource for exploring color relationships— geared directly toward fiber artists.*

Thomas, Heather. *A Fiber Artist's Guide to Color & Design.* Urbandale, IA: Landauer Publishing, 2011.

*A comprehensive guide to color and design study.*

Wells, Jean. *Intuitive Color & Design.* Lafayette, CA: C&T Publishing, 2009.

*Explore color and design from a quilt artist's point of view.*

Wolfrom, Joen. *Colorplay.* Lafayette, CA: C&T Publishing, 2000.

*Everything you need to know about color, with quilters in mind!*

Wolfrom, Joen. Studio Color Wheel. Lafayette, CA: C&T Publishing, 2010.

*Every studio needs this poster-size color wheel!*

Wolfrom, Joen. *Visual Coloring.* Lafayette, CA: C&T Publishing, 2007.

*Take the mystery out of choosing just-right colors and fabrics with the visual coloring technique.*

Wolfrom, Joen. Ultimate 3-in-1 Color Tool, updated 3rd edition. Lafayette, CA: C&T Publishing, 2010.

*Just what it says, in an easy-to-carry size.*

## Online Fabric Resources

**Blue Underground Studios, Inc.**
www.blueundergroundstudios.com

*Our website! Check us out for unique kits, including many silks and solid fabrics.*

**Hawthorne Threads**
www.hawthornethreads.com

*Great online fabric resource. Color grid provided for convenient shopping in one palette!*

**Quilt Home**
www.quilthome.com

*Quilt Home carries a variety of contemporary quilting fabrics. The website is user-friendly and the service is outstanding.*

**GloriousColor**
www.gloriouscolor.com

*Great source for Westminster prints, including those designed by Kaffe Fassett, Philip Jacobs, and Brandon Mably.*

**Fabricworm**
www.fabricworm.com

*Fresh, modern fabric for the person devoted to fabric.*

**Hancock's of Paducah**
www.hancocks-paducah.com

*A great one-stop shop for a multitude of fabric lines. Also a great place to shop for batiks and solids.*

**Fabric Shack**
www.fabricshack.com

*A good resource for jelly rolls, fat quarter packs, and batiks.*

## Fabric Attribution

*Bamboo quilt variation, pages 13 and 33: A Stitch in Color by Malka Dubrawsky for Moda Fabrics*

*Various collections, pages 35, 47, and 55, by Marcia Derse for Riverwoods by Troy*

# About the Authors

Amy Walsh

Amy has been sewing and quilting ever since she was old enough to sit at the sewing machine. As a little girl, she used to sneak down the stairs after bedtime to spy on her mother's sewing bees. She started her fabric collection at an early age by storing it in her bedroom closet.

Throughout her years of college and teaching, sewing, and especially fabric, remained her passion. In 2004, Amy left her job teaching history and started working as a longarm quilter. Amy started Blue Underground Studios, Inc., with fellow longarm quilter Janine Burke in 2005.

Amy resides in Chicago with her husband and two daughters.

Janine Burke

Janine's grandmother taught her to sew while she was in grade school. She spent many hours embroidering dish towels and pillowcases. Eventually her love of stitching led to a love of quilting, and she started collecting fabrics. After many years as a hobby quilter, Janine turned quilting into a career when she started longarm quilting. In addition to designing patterns, she also teaches classes and works in the industry in several different capacities. Janine resides in the Chicago area.

*Also by Amy Walsh and Janine Burke:*

Amy Walsh & Janine Burke

Colorful Quilts FOR FABRIC LOVERS

From Blue Underground Studios

10 Easy-to-Make Projects with a Modern Edge

# Great Titles and Products

## *from* C&T PUBLISHING *and* stashBOOKS.

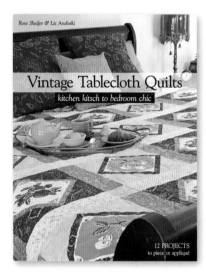

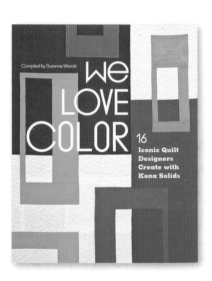

*Available at your local retailer or* **www.ctpub.com** *or* **800-284-1114**

For a list of other fine books from C&T Publishing, visit our website to view our catalog online.

**C&T PUBLISHING, INC.**

P.O. Box 1456
Lafayette, CA 94549
800-284-1114

Email: ctinfo@ctpub.com
Website: www.ctpub.com

C&T Publishing's professional photography services are now available to the public. Visit us at www.ctmediaservices.com.

**Tips and Techniques** can be found at www.ctpub.com > Consumer Resources > Quiltmaking Basics: Tips & Techniques for Quiltmaking & More

For quilting supplies:

**COTTON PATCH**

1025 Brown Ave.
Lafayette, CA 94549
Store: 925-284-1177
Mail order: 925-283-7883

Email: CottonPa@aol.com
Website: www.quiltusa.com

Note: Fabrics shown may not be currently available, as fabric manufacturers keep most fabrics in print for only a short time.